Access to History
General Editor: Keith Randell

The Concert of Europe: International Relations 1814–70

John Lowe

Hodder & Stoughton

A MEMBER OF THE HODDER HEADLINE GROUP

The cover illustration shows a portrait of Prince Metternich,
reproduced by gracious permission of Her Majesty the Queen.

Some other titles in the series:

France in Revolution   ISBN 0 340 53494 X
Duncan Townson
The Unification of Germany, 1815–79   ISBN 0 340 51810 3
Andrina Stiles
The Unification of Italy, 1815–70   ISBN 0 340 51809 X
Andrina Stiles
France: Monarchy Republic and Empire,   ISBN 0 340 51805 7
1814–70
Keith Randell
France: The Third Republic   ISBN 0 340 55569 6
Keith Randell
Rivalry and Accord: International Relations   ISBN 0 340 51806 5
1870–1914
John Lowe

British Library Cataloguing in Publication Data
Lowe, John *1934–*
  The concert of Europe: international relations 1814–70. –
  (Access to A-level History).
  1. Europe. Foreign relations, history
  I. Title   II. Series
  327.094

  ISBN 0 340 53496 6

First published 1990
Impression number 10 9 8 7 6 5
Year   1999 1998 1997 1996 1995 1994

Typeset by Wearset, Boldon, Tyne & Wear
Printed in Great Britain for Hodder & Stoughton Educational,
a division of Hodder Headline Plc, 338 Euston Road, London NW1 3BH
by Page Bros, Norwich.

Contents

Preface

To the general reader

Although the *Access to History* series has been designed with the needs of students studying the subject at higher examination levels very much in mind, it also has a great deal to offer the general reader. The main body of the text (i.e. ignoring the Study Guides at the ends of chapters) forms a readable and yet stimulating survey of a coherent topic as studied by historians. However, each author's aim has not merely been to provide a clear explanation of what happened in the past (to interest and inform): it has also been assumed that most readers wish to be stimulated into thinking further about the topic and to form opinions of their own about the significance of the events that are described and discussed (to be challenged). Thus, although no prior knowledge of the topic is expected on the reader's part, she or he is treated as an intelligent and thinking person throughout. The author tends to share ideas and possibilities with the reader, rather than passing on numbers of so-called 'historical truths'.

To the student reader

There are many ways in which the series can be used by students studying History at a higher level. It will, therefore, be worthwhile thinking about your own study strategy before you start your work on this book. Obviously, your strategy will vary depending on the aim you have in mind, and the time for study that is available to you.

If, for example, you want to acquire a general overview of the topic in the shortest possible time, the following approach will probably be the most effective:

1 Read Chapter 1 and think about its contents.
2 Read the 'Making notes' section at the end of Chapter 2 and decide whether it is necessary for you to read this chapter.
3 If it is, read the chapter, stopping at each heading or * to note down the main points that have been made.
4 Repeat stage 2 (and stage 3 where appropriate) for all the other chapters.

If, however, your aim is to gain a thorough grasp of the topic, taking however much time is necessary to do so, you may benefit from carrying out the same procedure with each chapter, as follows:

1 Read the chapter as fast as you can, and preferably at one sitting.
2 Study the flow diagram at the end of the chapter, ensuring that you understand the general 'shape' of what you have just read.

3   Read the 'Making notes' section (and the 'Answering essay questions' section, if there is one) and decide what further work you need to do on the chapter. In particularly important sections of the book, this will involve reading the chapter a second time and stopping at each heading and * to think about (and to write a summary of) what you have just read.

4   Attempt the 'Source-based questions' section. It will sometimes be sufficient to think through your answers, but additional understanding will often be gained by forcing yourself to write them down.

When you have finished the main chapters of the book, study the 'Further Reading' section and decide what additional reading (if any) you will do on the topic.

This book has been designed to help make your studies both enjoyable and successful. If you can think of ways in which this could have been done more effectively, please write to tell me. In the meantime, I hope that you will gain greatly from your study of History.

Keith Randell

CHAPTER 1

Introduction: Europe at the End of the Napoleonic Wars

1 The Revolutionary and Napoleonic Wars

The Revolutionary and Napoleonic wars which began in 1792 lasted until 1814, with only a brief interval of peace in 1802–3. By the time Napoleon finally accepted defeat, Europe had endured over 20 years of upheaval. Virtually every European state was affected by the conflict at one time or another. It involved states from Sweden in the north to Spain in the south and from Britain (and Ireland) in the west to Russia in the east. At one stage Turkey joined the anti-French coalition, while Napoleon's ambitions took him briefly to Egypt. France's colonies in the West Indies and the Indian Ocean (and those of her allies) were naturally regarded as fair game by Britain during the wars.

In such an extended and wide-ranging conflict there were few regions that completely escaped the devastation of war. Foreign armies trampled across the terrain, requisitioning food supplies and demanding billets from reluctant households. Many parts of Europe experienced occupation by French armies and were subjected to the insatiable demands of the tax collector and the recruiting sergeant. Traditional values and ways of life were under attack, frontiers were altered and rulers deposed.

Some of the changes that accompanied French rule, however, were regarded by many people as changes for the better. Serfdom was abolished, religious toleration was introduced and minorities, especially the Jewish communities, enjoyed much fairer treatment. French armies and officials were agents for the dissemination of the 'Principles of 1789' of the French Revolution. In regions adjacent to France ideals such as liberty, justice and careers open to talent were generally warmly welcomed, especially by the educated classes. Long after Napoleon's defeat, the Napoleonic Civil Code remained as a monument to French rationalism in many parts of Europe. Naturally, the traditional ruling classes were glad to see the end of French domination. More surprisingly, perhaps, many peasants and poorer townsmen were disillusioned with the liberation from tyranny which the French proclaimed as their mission. To a considerable extent the response varied according to region and social development. In more backward areas such as Spain, Naples and Russia, loyalty to God and King remained strong, whereas in the Low Countries, the Rhineland, North Italy and Switzerland French ideas were regarded, initially at least, as a liberation from arbitrary or obscurantist rule.

France declared war on Austria and Prussia in April 1792, although there was no pressing reason for hostilities at this particular time. There was some mistrust and suspicion on both sides, but the dominant political group in Paris exaggerated the threat to France while underestimating the risks of defeat. Above all, they mistakenly believed that war would consolidate their political position in France. For the next two years Revolutionary France was in danger of foreign invasion from a hostile Europe. From the autumn of 1794, however, the new French armies created by the revolutionary leaders, led by a new generation of very able generals, won a series of remarkable victories over the anti-French coalitions. A military genius had command of the French armies in Italy. Basing his novel tactics on the writings of military strategists published in the 1770s, Napoleon Bonaparte defeated the Austrians in 1796–7 and again in 1800. By then he had already seized power in France as First Consul (in November 1799), proclaiming himself Emperor in 1804. Faced with an impressive array of seemingly hostile states in 1804, Napoleon won a succession of spectacular victories against the armies of Austria, Prussia and Russia. By 1807 he was virtually the master of the European continent, sharing power only with the Tsar of Russia, but powerless to attack Britain after Nelson's great victory over the French and Spanish fleets at Trafalgar in 1805.

Napoleon's attempt to defeat the 'nation of shopkeepers' by economic warfare had disastrous results for him. The success of his 'Continental System' depended on closing all European ports to British ships – a formidable task, especially as Britain could retaliate by a virtual blockade of neutral commerce through her command of the seas. In seeking to control Portugal, French armies became involved in Spanish affairs which provoked a popular rising against them that turned into an exhausting guerrilla war, the 'Spanish ulcer'. The defence of Portugal provided Britain with a foothold on the continent whereby British forces, commanded by the future Duke of Wellington, could begin the destruction of French military power in Spain. The Continental System was also prone to evasion at Europe's northern extremity. It was largely Napoleon's determination to enforce the system against Russia, who was reluctant to sever trade with Britain, that led to his ill-fated Moscow campaign in 1812.

The French Empire was at its height in 1811, covering half a million square miles from Hamburg to Rome, and with a population of 44 millions (see map on page 20). As well as France itself, the French Empire included Belgium, Holland, the left bank of the Rhine, the north German coast, parts of Italy and 'Illyria' (along the Adriatic coast). These territories were governed from Paris and were subject to French law. However, the annexation of other states had not begun in the Napoleonic era – the only novelty was the scale on which it had taken place by 1811. Despite the so-called 'No Conquests' formula of the Revolutionary Assemblies, political leaders in the 1790s had annexed conquered regions to France (without waiting for an invitation), salving their consciences by reviving the concept of 'natural frontiers' which they applied particularly to the river Rhine.

In addition to the French Empire, Napoleonic Europe consisted of dependent states such as Spain, the rest of Italy, the Confederation of the Rhine and the Grand Duchy of Warsaw. With members of his family and victorious Marshals ruling many of these states, Napoleon was in danger of turning Europe into a sort of family business. Napoleon's power was also based on alliances with Denmark, Prussia and Austria. In short, Britain and Russia were the only significant states (apart from Turkey) outside Napoleon's orbit.

Napoleon threw all this away by his arrogant over-confidence in his ability to conquer Russia in a brief campaign, not unlike Hitler and his *blitzkrieg* in 1941. His Grand Army of over 500,000 men which invaded Russia in June 1812 was reduced to 100,000 by the time it reached Moscow in September. Less than one third of those remaining lived to retreat across the river Niemen into Poland in December 1812. The Moscow campaign was clearly a major factor in Napoleon's decline and fall.

2 The Defeat of Napoleon: Moscow to Waterloo via Leipzig, 1813–15

For much of 1813 diplomatic activity was more prominent than military exertion, as Russia and Prussia sought to bring Austria into a coalition against France. In August the Austrians finally declared war on France and put an army nearly 130,000 strong into the field. The decisive engagement came at Leipzig, the so-called 'Battle of the Nations' in October, when Napoleon's new army of 450,000 was defeated. Thereafter he could do little more than fight a succession of brilliant rearguard actions inside France until he was overwhelmed by force of numbers.

Napoleon's demise as Emperor of the French was brought about more by his own arrogance than by any united determination of the other Great Powers to dethrone him. His abdication in April 1814 was the direct outcome of his refusal to compromise and his reluctance to participate in peace negotiations on the basis of a reduction of French power to acceptable limits. In the course of 1813–14, the Great Powers became engaged in negotiations with each other to find a formula that would bring France to the conference table, without prejudice to their major interests. As a consequence, various commitments were entered into by the powers some time before France was actually defeated, some of which had an important influence on the peace treaties of 1814–15.

* In May 1813, a Russo-Prussian programme was agreed by which Austria and Prussia were to be restored to the strength they had had in 1805, while France would be allowed to keep her 'natural frontiers', but

See Preface for explanation of * symbol.

no more. It was not until August that Austria agreed to declare war on the French, and even then it was largely in the hope that it would convince Napoleon that he faced a united opposition, whose terms for peace he could not ignore. The hesitations of Metternich, the Austrian Foreign Minister since 1809, stemmed from an understandable desire to end the conflict while France was still strong enough to act as a counterweight to Russia (Russia's military power had grown enormously since the Moscow campaign). His other preoccupation was the future of the German states, which had been formed into a pro-French confederation by Napoleon. Prussian ministers had made several proposals for Germany which could be a serious threat to Austrian interests. It was therefore only after Metternich had failed to bring Britain into the negotiations, as well as failing to persuade Napoleon to come to terms, that Austria aligned herself with Russia and Prussia against France.

In the autumn of 1813 Britain decided to exert her influence in favour of a united front against Napoleon. Castlereagh, the Foreign Secretary, went over to the continent in January 1814 to stiffen the resolve of the allies to impose agreed terms on France. The disarray in the allied camp was quite startling. On the one hand Metternich was threatening to make a separate peace with Napoleon, while the Russian Tsar was threatening to march on Paris to depose him! After military reverses in February 1814, the Tsar accepted Castlereagh's demand that the allies conclude a preliminary treaty, binding themselves to joint action. In the Treaty of Chaumont (March 1814) the four powers agreed to continue the war until Napoleon accepted their terms and to maintain their alliance for a period of 20 years. The treaty also reiterated decisions taken earlier on the future of Holland, Spain, Italy, Germany and Switzerland.

Napoleon's unrealistic response to the allies sealed his fate. By the end of March allied troops had entered Paris, where leading French political figures were actively preparing to restore the Bourbon dynasty as a way of repudiating him. Napoleon's abdication in April 1814 and exile to the island of Elba (off the coast of Tuscany) with a generous pension, was expected to mark the end of the war. But his ambition and ego could not find adequate outlet in a tiny island and within a year he was back in France. Encouraged by reports of general disillusionment with the aged Bourbon king and of disaffection among the army, Napoleon escaped surveillance and landed in France in March 1815. His journey to Paris turned into a triumphant march as soldiers and Napoleonic officials rallied to his side. Marching into Belgium in early June, he checked the Prussian army sent against him, but he was out-generalled by Wellington, commanding a smaller force, at Waterloo. After his surrender, he was exiled to St Helena, an island 5,000 miles away in the mid-Atlantic, from which not even Napoleon could escape.

3 The Role of the Great Powers in the Defeat of France

During the whole period of the Revolutionary and Napoleonic wars the power which could claim the most consistent military commitment to the war effort against France was Austria. But she also had the dubious honour of having more armies beaten by the French than any of her allies. In terms of effective contributions to the defeat of France (and especially of Napoleon) the prize would be shared between Britain and Russia.

Britain became involved in the war against France in 1793 largely because the French occupation of Belgium and the expected invasion of Holland would place the whole coastline facing Britain in potentially hostile hands, threatening both her security and her trade. Lacking a large army or able commanders Britain's main contribution to the early coalitions against France took the form of financial subsidies and naval operations, such as Nelson's victory over the French fleet at the Battle of the Nile in 1798. Saved from invasion in 1804–5 by her island position and Nelson's destruction of the French and Spanish fleets at Trafalgar in 1805, Britain found herself alone against France once more by 1807. French intervention in Portugal and Spain led to the Peninsular War which played a major role in draining Napoleon's military resources, by tying up an army of 140,000 men by 1810. It also gave hope to other states by demonstrating that the French army was not invincible. Furthermore, Wellesley (later Duke of Wellington) built up an army of seasoned veterans who contributed to Napoleon's downfall with their victories in Spain in 1812–13. By this time the Fourth Coalition was being created, in which British diplomacy played a vital role. Castlereagh set about restoring the Grand Alliance, resulting in the Treaty of Chaumont (March 1814) in which Britain was to contribute not only financial subsidies but also an army of 150,000 men to the defence of Europe – a demonstration of Britain's recovery as a military power.

The Russian army available to resist Napoleon's invasion of Russia in 1812 was not much bigger than Britain's military commitment in the Treaty of Chaumont. Yet it was in the Moscow campaign that Russia made her greatest contribution to the defeat of France. Although Russian armies had played a prominent part in the Second and Third Coalitions against France, they had suffered almost as many reverses as the Austrians, with whom they were frequently at odds. Following further defeats in 1805–7, Tsar Alexander had concluded an alliance – not just a truce – with Napoleon at Tilsit, in which the two emperors divided the continent between them. The invasion of 1812 turned into a disaster for the French because the Russians refused to oblige Napoleon with the pitched battle he needed for a quick victory. Their strategic withdrawal and 'scorched earth' tactics lured the Grand Army, decimated by heat, disease and lack of food and water, to within 70 miles of

Moscow before they gave battle, on equal terms, at Borodino in September. On its retreat from Moscow, the tattered remnants of Napoleon's army were exposed to harassment by Russian forces and, finally, in December, to the ferocity of the Russian winter. The Moscow campaign destroyed the Grand Army and restored the reputation of the Russian army. From 1813 the new Russian army was the most formidable military force in Europe, playing a major role in Napoleon's defeat at the Battle of Leipzig (October 1813) and in subsequent campaigns. It was therefore a fitting symbol of Russia's role in the overthrow of Napoleon in 1814 that the Tsar, Alexander I, should enter Paris at the head of the victorious allied armies.

Prussia's role was a somewhat inglorious one. Although she, together with Austria, bore the brunt of the fighting against the revolutionary armies from 1792–5, her armies achieved only modest successes against the relatively inexperienced French forces. In 1795, Prussia abandoned the First Coalition in order to participate fully in the final partition of Poland. For the next decade, Prussia, under its weak and vacillating king, Frederick William III, took no real part in the war against France. Although she joined the Third Coalition in 1805, she soon secured a truce with France, only to be duped by Napoleon over his plans for Germany. Her attempt to protect her interests by declaring war ended in disaster when the Prussian army was crushed at the Battle of Jena in 1806. Some recovery took place during the period of reforms associated with the ministers Stein and Hardenberg, but Prussia found it expedient to make an alliance with France in early 1812. After Napoleon's retreat from Moscow Prussia changed sides, concluding the Treaty of Kalisch with Russia in early 1813. Her armies were thereafter committed to the allied war effort. In 1815, General Blucher's army was checked by Napoleon but survived to make a last-minute contribution to the Emperor's final defeat.

Austria's role in the wars against France was that of a more consistent and less unheroic opponent than Prussia. She was an active member of all the coalitions formed against France and her military contributions to the allied war effort were substantial, if not often crowned with success, especially against Napoleon. Encouraged by France's setbacks in Spain, the Austrians declared war only to be beaten again at Wagram in 1809, suffering territorial losses as a result. Like Prussia, she was allied to France in 1812 but after Napoleon's defeat in the Moscow campaign, Austrian policy became somewhat devious. However, Napoleon's ego frustrated Metternich's hopes for a negotiated peace with France, with the result that Austria turned to Britain for diplomatic support and agreed to the Treaty of Chaumont in March 1814.

4 The Great Powers after 1815: Political and Economic Factors

a) Great Britain

From the Battle of Waterloo to the outbreak of the Crimean War in 1854, Britain and Russia were the two dominant powers in international affairs. During this period of nearly 40 years they were, at times, engaged in rivalry for the diplomatic leadership of Europe, but they were also, on occasion, willing to act together to resolve problems of mutual concern, especially those arising from the decline of the Turkish Empire. In 1815, Britain was more than just supreme at sea – she had regained a reputation as a military power, thanks to Wellington's successes in Spain and his victory over Napoleon at Waterloo. Her financial strength had also enabled her to act as paymaster of the anti-French coalitions. For 50 years after 1815, Britain played an active and important part in European diplomacy. Although she was anxious to sustain the essentials of the peace settlement of 1814–15, Britain was not committed to a rigorous defence of the status quo, especially in matters concerning the smaller states.

As the 'First Industrial Nation', Britain enjoyed half a century or more of economic supremacy over her continental neighbours. As late as 1850, for example, she produced nearly five times as much coal as France and the two German powers combined. Her lead in manufacturing industry enabled her to dominate markets throughout the world: the United States, Latin America and India imported a large amount of Britain's manufactures, especially textiles and engineering goods, in exchange for food and raw materials. Europe was important to her, but only accounted for about one third of her total trade. Between 1840 and 1860 Britain's world trade trebled in value and continued to expand rapidly until the 1870s. In addition, the carrying trade of her merchant ships, her overseas investments and her banking and insurance services, which made London the financial centre of the world, all contributed to her growing prosperity. Her population, on the other hand, was almost absurdly small for a Great Power, rising from about 12 million in 1811 to 26 million in 1870. The combination of industrial and commercial strength, naval power and overseas empire made Britain unique amongst the Great Powers from 1815 to 1870.

Britain's political system was also unique in this period. In 1815 she possessed a well-established system of parliamentary government under a constitutional monarch who exercised some political influence, but who did not determine policy. This was the preserve of 'the Government' – the Prime Minister and other ministers, meeting as the Cabinet. The two main political parties, Whig and Tory (later Liberal and Conservative), could usually be distinguished by their policies and beliefs, despite their common aristocratic leadership – the Whigs being regarded as more progressive. In foreign affairs, similarly, Whigs tended to be more sympathetic than Tories to liberal movements abroad. But party allegiance was not the key factor that determined the attitude and policies of British foreign secretaries in this period. For example, Castlereagh (a Tory) and Palmerston (a Whig) shared the view that Britain should play an active part in the European Concert, while Canning, Castlereagh's successor, who was also a Tory, did not. Differences of temperament and personality were also more important than party differences in the contrast between 'Lord Pumicestone's' abrasive diplomacy and Lord Aberdeen's more relaxed and persuasive style from 1841 to 1846.

The political system in Britain was far from being democratic – even after the 1832 Reform Act only one in five adult males had the right to vote for Members of Parliament. But it was an open system of government, which took note of public opinion. Englishmen ('English' was used in the nineteenth century where nowadays 'British' would be appropriate) were proud of their liberties, which included freedom from arbitrary arrest, free speech and freedom of the press, all of which were virtually unknown in continental Europe in the early nineteenth century.

b) Russia

Russia's emergence as a European Great Power dated from her victories over Turkey and her acquisition of Polish territory in the late eighteenth century. Her reputation as a military power was greatly enhanced by the defeat inflicted on Napoleon's Grand Army in 1812–13, and by the maintenance of a large peacetime army. Until the mid-1850s, Tsarist Russia was a staunch defender of monarchical rights and conservatism but, following her defeat in the Crimean War of 1854–6, she became much less committed to maintaining the status quo in Europe.

The Russian economy was one of the most backward in Europe during the period 1815–70. Serfdom survived until 1861, embracing the majority of peasants who made up over 80 per cent of the total population of about 70 million at that date. The productivity of Russia's agriculture remained low before the colonisation of the more fertile Black Soil region of the south, while she scarcely counted as an industrial power before 1870. Until the creation of a railway system, which only began towards the end of this period, she could not effectively exploit her best sources of raw materials, which an unkind fate had sited hundreds of miles from her main population centres. This backward economy could scarcely provide the amount of revenue required by the state treasury of a Great Power. Russia was therefore a Great Power largely by virtue of her sheer size and the seemingly limitless supplies of serf conscripts for her armies.

Russia was ruled by an autocratic Tsar who, in theory, exercised unfettered power and was answerable to God alone. His authority, backed by the political police and the army, seemed unlimited but, in practice, there were several constraints upon it. At root, Tsarist Russia was a partnership between the Tsar and the landowning nobility and gentry whose interests could not be ignored. It was equally unwise for the Tsar to offend the higher clergy of the Orthodox Church, who sustained his image as God's representative on earth amongst the people. Nor was public opinion, despite censorship and control of the press, an entirely negligible factor. Above all, perhaps, the size of this vast multinational empire made it difficult to govern effectively, especially with a corrupt and incompetent bureaucracy – even though nationalism was not well developed in this period, except in Poland.

On the other hand, the Tsar was free to govern as an absolute ruler since no parliament existed before 1905. Ministers were his servants and although a Council of State and a Council of Ministers were created in 1810–12, their powers and functions were purely advisory. The same was true of foreign affairs, since although an able and experienced foreign minister such as Count Nesselrode (who served from 1815 to 1856) could exercise considerable influence over the direction taken by Russian foreign policy, it was the Tsar who decided important issues. The attitudes and personality of the Tsar were therefore significant factors in Russian policy. Alexander I (1801–25) abandoned his earlier liberal tendencies in 1820, while his successor Nicholas I (1825–55) was never troubled by such things, being an arch reactionary. Alexander II (1855–81), by contrast, seemed full of reforming zeal in the first half of his reign when he attempted to modernise Russian society and the economy.

c) France

Despite being the vanquished nation, France was nevertheless regarded after 1815 as ranking second only to Russia as a military power. With the rebuilding of her fleet she also became Britain's main rival as a naval power. During the reign of the restored Bourbons from 1815 to 1830, French diplomacy was equivocal. She contemplated an alliance with Russia as an escape from her exclusion from the 'victors' club' – the Quadruple Alliance of 1815. At the same time, her credentials as a champion of liberty in Europe made her hesitant over associating too closely with the other continental powers, who tended to regard her as the Revolution incarnate. The advent to power of a more liberal regime in France after the 1830 revolution offered an escape from this dilemma through a 'Liberal Alliance' with Britain. But Anglo-French cooperation in international affairs turned out to be a fitful matter from 1830 to 1870, partly because of British suspicions of French aims and partly through rivalry for prestige and trade.

France recovered well from the strain of the war, becoming a wealthy nation again with the advantages of a prosperous agriculture and flourishing trade. Her industrial growth, on the other hand, was spasmodic for several decades, following no clear pattern. Manufacturing industries organised on capitalist lines developed in some parts of the country, especially the north, but left other regions largely untouched. Consequently, much of France remained agricultural, with farming providing employment for about half the active population as late as 1870. Industrialisation only began to accelerate after 1850 when railway building and easy credit encouraged rapid expansion of the iron and steel industries. By this time her population growth had begun to decline dramatically. The rise in population from 27 million in 1801 to nearly 36 million in 1851 kept France ahead of all the other Great Powers except Russia, but by 1870 her population had become almost static, unlike the others.

France was the only continental power to have a system of government resembling that of Britain. The Charter of 1814 made France a constitutional monarchy in which the king retained considerable power and the right to vote was confined to the wealthy. But the revolution of 1830 brought about a change of monarch; that of 1848, a change of regime. The short-lived 'Republican Experiment' of 1848–51 introduced the principle of manhood suffrage, which remained thereafter the basis of the French electoral system. The 'democratic dictatorship' of Napoleon III (nephew of the great Napoleon) held sway from 1851 to 1870 but with some liberalisation of the system in the 1860s. Public opinion was a powerful force in French politics, as was the often irresponsible press, despite restrictions placed upon it. Administrative centralisation ensured that the will of Paris was enforced in the provinces through the prefects of the departments. The notion that Paris harboured an international revolutionary committee which plotted upheavals throughout Europe was, however, a fiction of the imagination of reactionaries, especially in Austria.

d) Austria

In the years from 1815 to 1848, Austria exerted an influence over European affairs that was quite out of proportion to her limited financial and military resources. This owed something to the astute diplomacy of her Foreign Minister, Prince Metternich. The main factor, however, was probably that Austria had several useful roles to play in international affairs: to keep Russia in check in eastern Europe; to maintain stability in central Europe (Germany and Italy); and to oppose the contagion of revolutionary ideas that was regarded as a threat to monarchical rule and conservatism.

Austria was the second largest European state, after Russia, with a population of over 30 millions in mid-century, comprising a dozen different nationalities. Her ability to act as a Great Power was undermined by military weakness, arising from a persistent financial crisis. Bankrupt in 1811, the Austrian treasury was burdened with a large national debt, the interest on which swallowed up about 30 per cent of the government's revenue from 1815 to 1848. The 'forest of bayonets', on which Metternich's policies were said to rely, was consequently sometimes little more than a wood – since half the army was often sent home on extended leave! The trebling of the national debt between 1848 and 1866 imposed such severe constraints on military expenditure that after 1858 the army lacked modern weapons – with dire results in 1866 when Austria faced the Prussian army. Although agriculture still employed 70 per cent of the population, manufacturing industry was showing signs of dynamism before 1848. This was most evident in Italian silk and cotton production and in the textile and engineering industries of Bohemia. In general, however, Austrian industry, much of which was sited in rural areas, was technologically backward, short of credit and fuel, and hampered by poor communications.

Austria was an absolute monarchy until the 1860s. She was ruled by an emperor who provided the sole unifying force in a multinational state. The Austrian Empire, artificially constructed out of provinces and former kingdoms and peopled by a dozen nationalities, seemed to be perennially on the verge of collapse. The main function of the Habsburg Emperor and his ministers was therefore to resist the forces of change by any means available. These included censorship, use of political police and reliance on a large bureaucracy and the army. Although regional assemblies were permitted, even introduced, they were just a harmless pastime for the landowning aristocracy, except in Hungary where the gentry fought hard to retain their hold over local government.

In Vienna (the Austrian capital) it was admitted that 'administration has taken the place of government'. A Council of State existed to advise the Emperor, but the overlapping responsibilities of departments and committees caused serious confusion. This, together with the Emperor's insistence on reading every document, created endless delays in decision-making. Changes in the system, following military defeat in 1859 and 1866, introduced a wide range of civil liberties and a form of parliamentary government, but the Emperor retained extensive powers, especially over the conduct of foreign policy. This was nothing new in Austria, since Francis I (d. 1835) had played an important part in the formulation of Austrian foreign policy, reinforcing Metternich's own reactionary tendencies. After the reign of the feeble-minded Ferdinand (1835–48), effective imperial rule was restored under Franz Joseph (d. 1918) whose main fault was his refusal to make timely concessions. His Foreign Minister in the 1850s, Count Buol, achieved the dubious fame of committing the 'almost inconceivable folly' of alienating Russia during the Crimean War. His successors were no more successful in coping with the challenge from Prussia after 1862.

e) Prussia

Prussia was regarded as the weakest of the five Great Powers in 1815. Hesitant and somewhat timid policies denied her the chance to exercise more influence over the smaller German states, where she tended to follow Austria's lead. This, combined with the respect felt by Frederick William III (d. 1840) for the Tsar, made her a willing member of the informal alliance of the so-called 'three Northern Courts' directed against revolutionary change in Europe. By 1870, however, Prussia had become a Great Power of the first rank. Astute commercial policies, followed by industrial development and military reform in the 1850s, provided the daring political leadership of the 1860s with the financial and military strength to alter the European balance of power decisively in Prussia's favour.

Prussia's territorial gains in 1815 in the Rhineland and Westphalia proved to be of great economic value to a previously impoverished, mainly agricultural state. The Rhenish textile industry was already a going concern in 1815 but the potential of the Rhine-Ruhr metal industry was not realised until the 1850s. Three factors played a crucial role in the expansion of the Prussian economy after 1850 – waterways, railways and the *Zollverein*. The *Zollverein*, or customs union, founded by Prussia in 1834 and joined by many other German states (except Austria) helped to reduce the problems that arose from Prussia's lack of territorial unity. Railways, canals and rivers, especially the Rhine, offered Prussian industry fast or cheap transport, of major importance to the Ruhr metal industry which depended on foreign ore. Prussia's industrial 'take-off', however, should not be ante-dated. In 1870 over 70 per cent of her population (which stood at 16 million in 1850) was still employed in agriculture, much as it had been in 1815. The foundations for Germany's future enormous industrial expansion were nevertheless being laid from 1850 and the Prussian government seems to have played a constructive role in this – a rare experience in nineteenth-century Europe.

Until the late 1840s Prussia was an absolute monarchy, despite the King's promise in 1815 to summon a representative assembly for the whole kingdom. Provincial assemblies and elected town councils existed, but all important decisions were taken by the King and his ministers in Berlin. Unlike Austria, however, the Prussian Council of State was organised on rational lines and the civil service was a model of efficiency. Then, in the late 1840s and early 1850s, Frederick William IV (1840–61) introduced political changes which made Prussia into a constitutional monarchy. This new regime carried out social reforms for the benefit of the peasantry and urban workers. The King and his

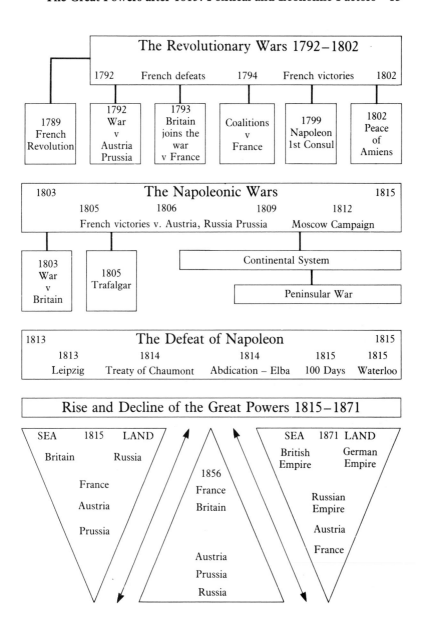

Summary – Europe at the End of the Napoleonic Wars

ministers still exercised wide powers and the electoral system was weighted heavily in favour of the wealthier classes, but despite this, the liberal opposition grew in strength and became involved in a constitutional conflict with the government over army reform and finance. In 1862 Otto von Bismarck was appointed Minister President to resolve this crisis. He failed in this, but his search for foreign policy successes had results for Prussia and for Europe that no one then envisaged.

***Making notes on** 'Introduction: Europe at the End of the Napoleonic Wars'*

The chapter you have just read is designed to provide you with the background information that will help you to understand the rest of the book. It contains information of two different types:

1. The first three sections attempt to provide you with a brief account of 'the story so far' by outlining the course of events in European international affairs between 1789 and 1815.
2. The fourth section provides a brief sketch of each of the five European Great Powers in 1815, followed by an indication of the major changes that took place in them up to 1870.

What is important is that you develop the general 'mental map' of the topic that you will need to carry with you as you read the chapters that follow. The notes you make should help you to acquire this. For this chapter you do not need to make the type of notes you will use for revision at a later stage. So any notes you make should be aids to learning rather than a record for future reference.

Very often it is only when you make yourself put ideas into words that they become clear in your mind. It is worth making notes as an aid to gaining that clarity. For example, look at the Summary diagram on page 13. Write down one sentence to summarise each of the six elements of the diagram. The six ideas you formulate in this way will form the basis of your 'mental map'.

Divide a sheet of paper into five equal-width columns. Write down the names of the Great Powers as the headings for the columns. Under each name write down one or two phrases in answer to each of the following four questions. You may not be able to find answers in all cases. Ask yourself why.

1. What were its main strengths in 1815?
2. What were its main weaknesses in 1815?
3. What changed during the period 1815–70?
4. What were its main interests in international affairs during the period 1815–70?

Now you should be well equipped to tackle the rest of the book.

CHAPTER 2

The Congress of Vienna

1 Introduction

The diplomatic negotiations at Vienna from the autumn of 1814 to the summer of 1815 took place amidst scenes of glittering splendour. The Austrian Emperor provided hospitality on a lavish scale for the royalty and aristocrats representing the states of Europe. While they attended banquets, balls and dramatic entertainments, Metternich's secret police examined the contents of their waste paper baskets to provide him with the latest inside information on the political intentions, not to mention the romantic intrigues, of his important guests.

The most prestigious delegation at the Congress of Vienna was the one from Russia. It was headed by Tsar Alexander, whose fine bearing and charming manner made him an impressive figure. He surrounded himself with a remarkably cosmopolitan group of advisers, including the very liberal-minded 'Greek' (from Corfu), John Capodistrias, who had been in Russian service since 1809. The diversity of the Tsar's entourage exacerbated the difficulty of predicting what line he would take. Alexander was a complex and unpredictable character, whose liberal inclinations were at odds with both his religious piety and his authoritarian tendencies. On one point, however, the Tsar did not waver. This was his *idée fixe* of restoring a large Polish state with a liberal constitution, with himself as King. Frederick William III of Prussia was indecisive and prone to succumb too readily to Alexander's charm (and his Polish scheme) so his chief minister, Prince Hardenberg, had an important role to play in the negotiations. Prussia's main interest was territorial expansion in north Germany, at the expense of Saxony.

Austrian interests were ably defended by Prince Metternich, a Rhinelander who became Habsburg Foreign Minister in 1809 (and State Chancellor from 1821). Metternich prided himself on his cultivated, aristocratic tastes, but contemporaries had a low opinion of his honesty. Napoleon, for example, objected that while everyone lied sometimes, Metternich lied all the time! His determination to suppress revolutions earned him the accusation: 'Never was a man more feared or detested than Metternich'. At Vienna, his priority was to re-establish Austrian power and influence in central and eastern Europe against Russia.

The British delegation was headed by Lord Castlereagh, the Foreign Secretary from 1812 to 1822. He was a handsome, aristocratic but rather aloof figure. Although he became unpopular in Britain because of his association with repressive Tory policies after the war, in 1814 he was admired and trusted by the allied leaders on the continent with whom he had already worked closely for about 18 months. He had played a major part in the formation of the Fourth Coalition. The aim of the British delegation was to create barriers against expansion by either France or Russia. It was also hoped that all maritime and colonial issues would be excluded from discussion at the Congress, for fear of criticism of Britain's wartime conduct at sea and extensive colonial gains.

France was represented by Talleyrand, a former bishop of the old regime turned wily diplomat, who served successive regimes after 1789. But he managed to keep his head. As he said, 'I have never conspired except when I had the majority of France for my accomplice'. He had been foreign minister from 1799 to 1807, but he had disapproved of Napoleon's more grandiose ambitions. As the spokesman for the restored Bourbon monarchy, he was a keen advocate of the principle of 'legitimacy'. His main aim at the Congress was to secure a place for France in the deliberations of the victorious Great Powers.

* The 'Vienna Settlement' consisted of three sets of negotiations. In the First Treaty of Paris (May 1814) the allies made peace with France after Napoleon's abdication and agreed the main features of the settlement for western Europe. At the Congress of Vienna (October 1814 to June 1815) a settlement for central and eastern Europe was laboriously thrashed out. After Napoleon's return to France and renewal of hostilities, ending in his defeat at Waterloo, the allies presented France with more severe demands in the Second Treaty of Paris (November 1815). The Congress of Vienna was originally intended to be little more than a formal ratification of the Treaty of Paris, but it turned out to be a major stage in the process of peacemaking.

The victorious Great Powers, Russia, Prussia, Austria and Britain, had intended to limit discussion of major issues to themselves, but they were persuaded by Talleyrand to accord recognition to a Committee of Eight, which included France, Sweden, Spain and Portugal, who had also been signatories of the First Treaty of Paris in May 1814. Although this Committee of Eight met quite frequently, the major territorial issues were decided by the Great Powers themselves, who set up sub-committees to deal with particular problems. But when a serious rift developed among the Great Powers in late 1814, Talleyrand seized the opportunity to align France with Britain and Austria and thus secured a voice in the deliberations – at least until Napoleon's return to France destroyed Talleyrand's credibility.

Historians have noted similarities in the procedures of the peace conferences of 1815 and 1919. For example, in 1919 major issues were decided by a Council of Four, assisted by specialist commissions, meeting alongside a less important Council of Ten. However, a major difference was that the participation of the defeated nation in the peace conferences of 1814–15 was not repeated in 1919 with respect to Germany.

2 Problems Facing the Peacemakers

A major problem facing the peacemakers in 1814–15 was the chaos caused by 22 years of war and the overthrow of regimes and frontiers. Europe was in a real sense like 'a world turned upside down'. Since 1792 and, more especially, since 1805, enormous changes had been made to the map of Europe. In central Europe the frontiers of Austria, Prussia and the smaller German states had been drastically re-shaped. Italy had also undergone numerous alterations. Some states had been annexed to France, while others had been grouped and later regrouped into republics, then kingdoms. In eastern Europe, Poland – which had ceased to exist in 1795 after its final partition between Russia, Austria and Prussia – had been partially resurrected by Napoleon as the Grand Duchy of Warsaw. Rulers as well as peoples had been subjected to the whims of Napoleon the conqueror. The Bourbons were deposed from the throne of Spain, while two of Napoleon's generals, Murat and Bernadotte, became rulers respectively of Naples and Sweden. Consequently, the peacemakers were confronted with a host of questions to be decided regarding state boundaries and rulers (see maps on pages 18 and 20).

    * Probably the most important problem facing the peacemakers was how to prevent France from overrunning neighbouring states and disturbing the peace of Europe in future. Most of the states bordering France in the 1790s had been too small and too weak to offer effective resistance to French armies. However, a solution to the problem was reached fairly easily, since the victorious Great Powers were in complete agreement on the need to 'contain' France, in contrast to the strong disagreements that arose on other issues.

One of these was the fate of the German states – a contentious issue between Austria and Prussia since 1813. It remained to be decided what sort of federal structure should replace Napoleon's Confederation of the Rhine, which had itself taken the place of the Habsburg-dominated Holy Roman Empire. However, the most serious disagreement that arose at Vienna was over the future of Poland. The Tsar proposed to create a large independent Poland, with himself as King, to replace Napoleon's Grand Duchy of Warsaw which had been created out of territory acquired by Prussia and, to a lesser extent, Austria in the 1790s. This plan was presented to the allies as a sort of moral obligation, precluding discussion. In terms of practical politics, however, the independence of 'Congress Poland', as it came to be called, was illusory – the reality was that it would be a Russian satellite. The Polish question therefore had serious implications for the European balance of power. It also affected the balance of power in Germany, because Prussia was keen to acquire Saxony (a German state) as compensation for the Polish territory she would forfeit.

The treatment of France became a major problem only after the

Free Cities:

B Bremen

F Frankfurt

H Hamburg

L Lübeck

—— Boundary of Holy Roman Empire

→ Dependent territory

M = Milan

G = Genoa

☐ Prussian territories

100 mls
160 km

Central Europe in 1789

'Hundred Days'. In 1814, after Napoleon's abdication, Castlereagh had persuaded the other victors without much difficulty to accept his case that leniency towards France was the best guarantee for the survival of the Bourbon regime and, by extension, for stability in Europe. But after Napoleon's triumphant return to France in 1815 and the flight of Louis XVIII to Brussels, Castlereagh's assurances seemed somewhat hollow. Russia and, to a lesser extent, Austria demanded a punitive peace while the Prussians and some of the German states clamoured for the dismemberment of France.

Finally the 'restlessness of the masses' might be deemed to have been a problem for the statesmen at Vienna. Since 1795 French armies had spread an awareness of the ideas of liberty and equality and, after 1805, the concepts of the Napoleonic Civil Code. In addition, the French occupation of Europe, increasingly severe in its demands on the civilian population, had provoked some stirrings of patriotic and nationalistic feeling. Such ideologies could not easily be accommodated to the Great Powers' conception of the need for peace and order in Europe.

3 Aims and Principles

In recent years some historians have become dissatisfied with the traditional way of presenting the aims and principles of the Vienna Settlement. For example, it is commonly stated that the Vienna Settlement was based on the twin principles of 'legitimacy' and 'the balance of power'. A variant on this is the assertion that the avowed intention of the Congress was 'Restoration founded on Legitimacy'. To this could be added a third principle, 'rewards for the victors', with the 'containment of France', a 'fundamental aim' of the settlement, as a fourth. Such assertions are not so much incorrect as misleading, because they oversimplify a complex situation. In the first place, it seems that the peacemakers only recognised the claims of former rulers when it suited them. Secondly, although all the Great Powers did attach importance to the concept of the balance of power, they tended to interpret it to suit their own national interests. It therefore lacked a precise meaning.

It might be more helpful to an understanding of the Vienna Settlement, therefore, to recognise that it represented a series of compromises by the Great Powers, whose views were by no means identical. Important differences of opinion had characterised most of the negotiations among the allies since 1813. Metternich, for example, was far from convinced before 1814 that it made sense to destroy Napoleon's power in western Europe if the result was to leave Russia dominating the continent. This explains why Castlereagh had insisted on the need for a united front in both diplomacy and war in dealing with Napoleon, which was eventually agreed in the Treaty of Chaumont (March 1814). What the Great Powers had in common, of

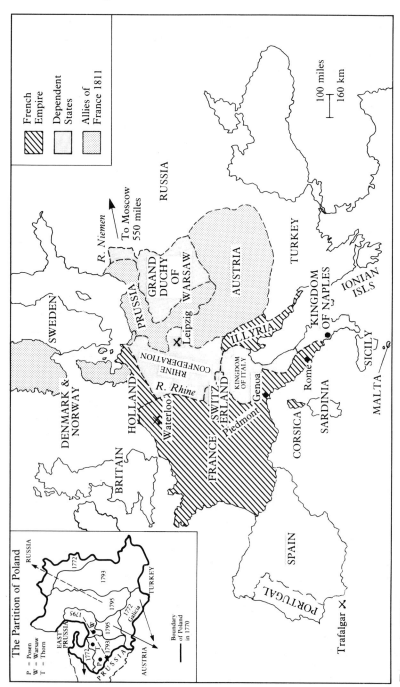

Europe in 1811

course, in 1813–15 was a desire for peace, security and stability, but they did not necessarily agree on the best means to achieve the desired end. This was still the case in 1815, as is shown in the arguments over whether to treat France with leniency again after the Battle of Waterloo.

Underlying the whole process of peacemaking in 1814–15, and exercising considerable influence over the outcome of the Congress was the fact that a series of treaties had been concluded among some or all of the allies before 1814. For example, in the Treaty of Kalisch (February 1813) Russia made specific promises on Prussia's right to recover her former strength as a Great Power. Other commitments were made by the Great Powers in the course of their attempts to force Napoleon to the conference table, culminating in the Treaty of Chaumont. Although primarily a military alliance intended to last for 20 years, secret articles re-affirmed decisions previously taken regarding Holland, Spain, Italy, Switzerland and Germany.

The fact that the peacemakers did not start with a 'clean slate' explains why some historians in recent years have tended to play down the role of 'principles' in the Vienna Settlement. Instead they have emphasised the importance of these previous commitments and regard the settlement as based on pragmatic, rather than doctrinaire, considerations related to the different situations which prevailed in western Europe and in central and eastern Europe.

In western Europe, priority was naturally given to ways of restraining France from territorial expansion in the future. This was to be achieved by offering the defeated nation lenient peace terms, by strengthening the states on France's borders and by renewing the alliance of the allied powers. Much of the territorial settlement in western Europe, agreed in principle at the First Treaty of Paris in March 1814, was designed to meet the strategic requirements of the policy of 'containing' France.

The territorial settlement in central Europe was also influenced, to some extent, by strategic considerations since it was necessary to strengthen Prussia along the Rhine and Austria in north Italy. Apart from this, a variety of factors was at work. For instance, Austria was entitled to compensation for the loss of the Austrian Netherlands and frontiers had to be tidied up after the confusion caused by frequent boundary changes over the previous 20 years. 'Rough justice' was meted out in the form of rewards to those rulers who had abandoned Napoleon to join the allies in good time, while punishing the laggards, such as Saxony and Denmark.

 * The concept of the balance of power was invoked most vigorously in the context of the settlement of central and eastern Europe, which gave rise to serious disagreements among the peacemakers. In British and Austrian eyes, Russia's claim to Poland threatened the balance of power in Europe as a whole, while Prussian claims to all of Saxony were a threat to the balance of power within Germany. In the event, Russia

remained too powerful but a sort of balance was achieved between the two German powers by Austria's acquisition of territory and influence in Italy, to match Prussia's gains in Germany itself. In this sense, the balance of power was an important principle behind the Vienna Settlement, though Castlereagh and Metternich doubted whether they had succeeded in achieving a 'just equilibrium'.

* 'Legitimacy' was also invoked as a principle in the peace settlement but its application was haphazard. Former dynasties were restored when it suited the convenience or the interests of one or more of the Great Powers, but a legitimate ruler such as the King of Saxony was threatened with dispossession of his territory in order to satisfy Prussian claims. The main exponent of the principle was Talleyrand, who had advocated the restoration of the Bourbons to France in 1814, at which time the Tsar preferred Bernadotte of Sweden or even a republic. At Vienna, Talleyrand invoked legitimacy to press the claims of Ferdinand I of Naples to his former throne, in order to evict Murat (a Napoleonic appointment) to whom Metternich was obligated by treaty. In most cases where the principle of legitimacy appears to have been applied there was another consideration at work. In the case of Spain, for example, the restoration of the Bourbon dynasty, displaced by Napoleon in 1808, seemed only natural justice to an ally. In central Italy, restoring Habsburg dukes and princesses was part of Metternich's design to create an Austrian paramountcy over Italy and to keep French influence at bay. All in all, the evidence suggests that the allied leaders did not regard legitimacy as a very compelling principle.

If one looks back over the peace settlement it is possible to identify a number of 'principles' which seem to have had some influence over the decisions taken in 1814–15. The point that some modern historians emphasise, however, is that the statesmen arrived at the conference table with a series of prior agreements and treaties, rather than a set of principles, which they expected to be endorsed. The task confronting the peacemakers was therefore the practical one of trying to reconcile these existing agreements with the overall aim of creating a stable order in western, central and eastern Europe.

Finally, it seems clear that the Great Powers felt it was their right and duty to re-establish the law of nations against the dictates of a conqueror. Consequently they acted as if this entitled them to claim a right of protection over the smaller states, without necessarily consulting them. The aim they set themselves (which they believed only Great Powers could achieve) was to re-establish a world where order, not war and revolution, prevailed.

4 The Territorial Settlement

The Great Powers' desire for peace, security and order – order within states as well as between states – was demonstrated in the territorial settlement made in 1814–15. Despite all the changes, it is sometimes asserted that the map of Europe in 1815 represented, with only minor qualifications, a return to the pre-war status quo. The validity of this statement can be judged by a comparison of the map of Europe in 1789 with that of 1815 (see pages 18 and 25).

In western Europe, the key factor in the territorial settlement was the 'containment' of France, which necessitated the re-drawing of state boundaries. In central Europe, the future of the Italian states and Germany had to be decided in conjunction with the territorial interests of Austria and Prussia. It was here that the peacemakers most clearly revealed their limited vision, missing the opportunity to satisfy aspirations for good government and some viable form of national identity. In eastern Europe, the crucial issue was the size and shape of the Kingdom of Poland which the Tsar was determined to create – seemingly by force, if necessary.

* The solution adopted to deal with the weakness of France's immediate neighbours was to create more powerful 'buffer' states on her borders. The areas most easily overrun by French armies since the 1790s had been the Austrian Netherlands (Belgium), the Rhineland and the coastal strip of north Italy. It was decided therefore to join Belgium and Holland together under the Dutch king as the United Netherlands, whose frontiers were to be reinforced by restoring the old 'barrier fortresses'. In the Rhineland, Prussian territory was greatly extended and Bavaria and Baden were also strengthened. The independence and neutrality of Switzerland, a route into central Europe for French armies, were recognised by all the Great Powers, including France. To close the gap into north Italy, the formerly independent republic of Genoa was incorporated into Piedmont, which was further enlarged by the restoration of Nice and most of Savoy. With Prussian forces ready to be deployed along the Rhine or to assist the King of Holland and Austrian armies in Lombardy, to the east of Piedmont, France was surrounded by a 'cordon sanitaire' which would severely restrict her opportunities to expand in future.

* The territorial settlement in Italy illustrates the limited vision of the statesmen at Vienna in that, for the most part, they revived the pre-war system of separate sovereign states and restored the old dynasties. A federal union, taking account of regional loyalties, would have been an appropriate political structure for Italy, whose people hoped for something better than the arbitrary, despotic regimes foisted on them in 1815. However, it has to be recognised that the frequent changes in boundaries initially made by France between 1797 and 1811 were not inspired by an altruistic desire to promote the unification of the peninsula. Those changes had no particular logic to them and were based largely on expediency – the fiscal and manpower needs of the French regime. Accordingly, by 1811, some Italian states had been annexed outright to the French Empire, while others had been formed

into the Kingdom of Italy. Only Naples resembled its former identity, but under the rule of Murat, a Napoleonic general.

At first sight, the reconstitution of the Italian states gives the appearance of being based on four 'principles' – the containment of France, territorial compensation, the balance of power and legitimacy. In fact, the Italian settlement was designed to serve Austrian interests. She secured Lombardy (centred on Milan) and acquired Venetia, a former independent republic, as compensation for the loss of the Austrian Netherlands. She also acquired the Adriatic possessions of the Venetian Republic, including Dalmatia. Austrian influence was further increased by the restoration of Habsburg rulers to the central duchies of Parma, Modena and Tuscany. The restoration of the old regime in Italy was symbolised by the return to the Pope of the Papal States, garrisoned by Austrian troops. Ferdinand I's recovery of Naples, demanded by Talleyrand in the name of legitimacy, was facilitated by King Murat's ill-judged decision to side with Napoleon after his escape from Elba. This enabled Metternich to ignore his treaty obligations to Murat (made in early 1814), while securing from Ferdinand a promise not to grant his subjects a constitution.

The Vienna Settlement created an Austrian paramountcy in Italy to the exclusion of French influence. This was blatant Great Power politics, which recognised Austria's entitlement to compensation and her supporting role to the 'buffer' state of Piedmont on the French frontier. Her Italian gains were supposed to strengthen her as a Great Power, vital to European stability, and to act as a counterweight to the aggrandisement of Prussia in Germany.

* The re-shaping of Germany in 1814–15 provides another example of the limited vision and pragmatism of the peacemakers. On the one hand they accepted the logic of Napoleon's drastic reduction in the number of sovereign states of the old Holy Roman Empire, but they failed to endow the new Germany with a coherent structure or viable constitution. As in the case of Italy, the peacemakers were faced with the confusion that France had caused by changing state boundaries to suit French interests. Some parts of Germany had been annexed to France, some states had been truncated (such as Prussia) while others had been enlarged, and totally new amalgamations had been created, such as the Kingdom of Westphalia, without any overall rationale.

The basic decision to set up a new German Confederation of 39 states made sense, but it perpetuated the existence of too many weak, small states. At one extreme the Confederation included the two German Great Powers, Austria and Prussia, while at the other extreme were the four Free Cities: Hamburg, Lübeck, Bremen and Frankfurt. In the north, Hanover was elevated to the status of a kingdom. In the south, Bavaria gained valuable additions of territory (including the Palatinate), strengthening the Rhine frontier, in exchange for territory restored to Austria. The German Confederation also included within its boundaries

Central Europe in 1815

two duchies, Holstein and Luxemburg, ruled by the kings of Denmark and Holland respectively, which became a cause of contention in the 1860s.

If the opportunity existed to make Germany a more powerful force in European affairs, as Castlereagh wished, it was not taken in 1815. The kingdoms, dukedoms and Free Cities enjoyed equal rights as independent sovereign states, sending non-elected representatives to a Diet at Frankfurt, under an Austrian president. The new Germany largely reflected Metternich's desire for a weak federation, dominated by Austria. Proposals made by Stein and Hardenberg in 1813 for a single sovereign German state, or for a north/south division of influence between Prussia and Austria were strongly opposed by Metternich.

Although the restoration of Austria to her 1805 strength had been agreed without difficulty, facilitated by Bavaria's willingness to return territorial gains, the reconstruction of Prussia was much more contentious. This was because Prussian claims were linked to a much larger issue, which brought the allies to the brink of war against each other. The root of the problem was Tsar Alexander's determination to establish a large Polish state as a Russian satellite and to compensate Prussia for the loss of her former Polish territory with the whole of Saxony. This had been the essence of the Treaty of Kalisch ((February 1813) by which Prussia agreed to abandon its alliance with France and to side with Russia against Napoleon.

From Austria's point of view, the strategic implications of this Russo-Prussian deal were very serious. Russian influence would be extended further west into Europe, while Prussia would be well placed to dominate north Germany, especially if she also secured the major fortress of Mainz. But, as both Poland and Saxony were occupied by Russian troops at the end of the war, Russia was in an almost impregnable position. The gravity of the situation is shown by the fact that at one stage Castlereagh had even feared that the Tsar would not bother to attend the Congress at Vienna but would simply dictate terms – on the basis of 'possession being nine-tenths of the law'. Castlereagh had also visited Paris en route for Vienna in August 1814 to enquire 'whether France was prepared to support her views on the Polish question by arms?' He hoped to solve the problem by persuading Prussia to stand firm with Austria in opposition to the Tsar's plans for Poland, in return for the whole of Saxony. This stratagem failed, however, when the somewhat timid Prussian King quailed before the Tsar's angry outbursts and ordered his minister, Hardenberg, to cease cooperating with Castlereagh and Metternich.

This rift amongst the victorious powers in late 1814 gave Talleyrand just the opportunity he needed to assert French influence at the Congress. Reinforcing Metternich's own anxieties over the effect on the balance of power of a Prussian acquisition of the whole of Saxony, he encouraged him to stand firm on the issue. When Prussia threatened war in December 1814, Talleyrand agreed to participate with Britain and Austria in the tripartite alliance against Prussia and Russia – without demanding concessions for France in return. Faced with this show of strength, the Russo-Prussian front collapsed in January 1815, allowing Castlereagh to negotiate a compromise solution which preserved a balance between the two German powers. Prussia secured about two-fifths of Saxony (40 per cent of its population, 60 per cent of its land) and a larger area of Polish territory, including Posen and Thorn.

Once this major crisis was over, the Great Powers were able to proceed with the disposition of other territories. The Ionian Islands in the Adriatic, formerly belonging to the Venetian Republic, were placed under British protection. Sweden acquired Norway from Denmark (who paid the price of staying loyal to Napoleon too long) – a transfer agreed in 1812 to compensate Sweden for the loss of Finland, occupied by Russia since 1808.

By 1815, Russia had become a much more formidable force in international affairs, advancing her western frontier several hundred miles forward into Europe (see maps on pages 18 and 25). She had obtained large amounts of Polish territory in the Partitions of 1793 and 1795 and was set to dominate 'Congress Poland' after 1815. She had also acquired Finland and gained Bessarabia from her latest war with Turkey, which had ended with the Treaty of Bucharest in 1812. Prussia likewise obtained valuable additions of territory, consolidating her previously scattered possessions in the Rhineland and Westphalia. For Austria the main benefit of the peace settlement was the recovery of territory forfeited after her earlier defeats by Napoleon, and the consolidation of her power base in Italy. Britain's gains were made overseas. She retained Tobago, St Lucia and Mauritius, taken from France, as well as Ceylon and Cape Colony taken from Holland, for which she paid financial compensation, earmarked for the repair of the barrier fortresses.

  ★ France got off lightly. The victorious allies were remarkably lenient towards the state that had created such upheavals in Europe since 1792. This peace of reconciliation was another aspect of 'containing' France by re-integrating her into the European states system. In the First Treaty of Paris (May 1814) she kept her 1792 frontiers, as well as the art treasures looted from all over Europe by Napoleon. No indemnity or army of occupation was imposed. However, France was required to give her assent to a series of changes which the allies envisaged making in Europe. These related to Holland, Germany, Switzerland and Italy in particular, as well as Britain's acquisition of various islands. But Britain actually returned far more overseas prizes than she kept.

Even after Napoleon's ill-fated return from Elba, France was saved from the punitive peace terms which Holland and some of the German states, especially Prussia, wished to impose on her. By the Second Treaty of Paris (November 1815) her frontiers were slightly reduced by fixing them at their 1790 limits. She had also to pay an indemnity of 700 million francs, a substantial sum, and return the stolen art treasures, as well as suffer an army of occupation for three to five years. Napoleon himself was exiled to St Helena, a distant island in the south Atlantic. Even so, these were not harsh terms for a nation which had seemingly welcomed Napoleon's return and had therefore to accept some measure of responsibility for disturbing the peace of Europe yet again, before the peace settlement, commenced in May 1814, was even completed. Castlereagh, with some support from Metternich, demonstrated his statesmanship by his insistence that European peace and stability would not be secure if France was resentful. Instead of weakening France, the allies sought to strengthen the bonds uniting them against a repetition of French aggression. In November 1815, in the Treaty of Defensive Alliance (often called the Quadruple Alliance), they renewed the pledges made to each other in the Treaty of Chaumont (March 1814). They agreed to uphold the terms of the Second Treaty of Paris and to resist by force the return to France of Napoleon or one of his family. An important addition to this renewal of the Treaty of Chaumont was Article VI which provided for periodic meetings of the allies to consider measures to maintain the peace of Europe. It was this article which provided the formal basis for the Congress System.

As well as re-drawing the map of Europe, the Great Powers also signed a number of general agreements. The perpetual neutrality of the Swiss Confederation, consisting of 22 cantons (states) was agreed. The navigation of rivers which flowed through several countries was declared open to all commerce, on which duties were not to be increased. In such measures the Great Powers were attempting to establish the existence of a 'public law' for all European states. A British attempt to obtain an immediate ban on the slave trade from Africa to the Americas was unsuccessful, but France promised to prohibit the trade within five years. However, Spain and Portugal insisted on the need for a longer interval of time before they could attempt to enforce a measure which would have a disruptive effect on the economies of some of their colonies in the West Indies and South America.

5 Success or Failure?

The Vienna Settlement attracted more criticism than praise for much of the nineteenth century. Many of Metternich's contemporaries were certainly far from impressed with the work of the Congress, as is shown in this comment by Metternich's principal adviser, von Gentz:

1 The Congress has resulted in nothing but restorations which had

already been effected by arms, agreements between the Great
Powers of little value for the preservation of the peace of Europe,
quite arbitrary alterations in the possessions of the smaller states,
5 but no act of a higher nature, no great measure for public order or
the general good which might compensate humanity for its long
suffering or pacify it for the future.

These themes were elaborated in a pamphlet published in Britain in
1821 which complained that after Napoleon's defeat:

1 ... we saw with satisfaction the opportunity return to Europe of
repairing its many losses, and of regaining the liberties of which
its People had for long been deprived. But these hopes were
disappointed. Treaties indeed were made, with more or less
5 regard to an imaginary standard, by which the territorial possessions of certain great states were to be balanced against each other
... but neither in settling the treaties of 1814 or 1815, nor at the
subsequent congresses at Aix-la-Chapelle and Carlsbad, does it
appear that any regard was to be had to the only basis on which,
10 in the present condition of the world, the Peace could be
consolidated, to the solemn promises of the Sovereigns in the
hour of their necessity, nor to the Rights which the People of
Europe had acquired for themselves at the expense of so many
sacrifices and sufferings ... Public opinion was disregarded.
15 National feeling was despised, and the expression of it harshly
repulsed. Whole countries were transferred from one Prince to
another, without any consideration for the wishes or habits, or the
ancient prejudices under which they had lived happy and become
great.

The fact that the period from 1815 to 1848 is often referred to as 'The
Age of Revolutions' strongly suggests that the Vienna Settlement failed
to achieve the aim of re-establishing order within states. In the late
nineteenth century, it was commonly asserted that the 'reactionaries' of
1815 resolutely set their faces against the new forces of the age –
Liberalism and Nationalism. Furthermore, it was asserted that the
principle of legitimacy was invoked to justify the return of 'discredited
dynasties' in Spain, Italy and Germany, whose despotic rule provoked
revolutions in the following decades. Typical of this approach is the
comment of a French historian writing in the 1890s to the effect that the
Vienna statesmen rejected the aspirations of the people for free
institutions and the clamour of nations for independence and natural
frontiers. This critical attitude persits even among modern French
historians who continue to condemn 1815 as 'the triumph of reaction'.
The peace settlement has also been attacked for the exclusion of the
smaller powers from decision-making. By arrogating to themselves the

right to decide the fate of smaller states, the Vienna statesmen, it is said, put too high a premium on international stability at the expense of the wishes and aspirations of peoples. Cavour, the Prime Minister of Piedmont in 1852, commented in 1846:

1 Resting on no principle, neither that of legitimacy, nor of national interests, nor of popular will, taking account neither of geographical conditions, nor of general interests, this august assembly, acting only by right of the strongest, erected a political edifice
5 without any moral foundation.

The reluctance of the Vienna statesmen to favour constitutional government in the smaller states is generally regarded as a major flaw in the settlement of 1814–15. If Metternich could hardly be expected to tolerate the creation of republics after the experience of the Reign of Terror in France, his insistence on restoring monarchical rule without any checks on the abuse of royal power was unduly rigid. Even so, despite Metternich's strong antipathy to liberalism, constitutions were introduced in several European states. France enjoyed the benefits of The Charter of 1814, 'the most liberal form of government to be found in Europe at that time'. Constitutions were also granted in some of the German states, in accordance with the terms under which the Confederation was established in 1815. Overall, though, it has to be conceded that the opportunity to make provision for better government in the smaller states was missed.

With regard to nationalism, on the other hand, it may be argued that the peacemakers cannot be fairly criticised for their neglect of it in 1815. Certainly, some historians have argued that if nationalist feelings had been allowed fuller expression after 1815, Europe could have been spared many of the wars and upheavals engendered by nationalism later on in the century. Others, however, have suggested that the emergence of an aggressive, expansionist nationalist feeling in the later nineteenth century demonstrates the potentially disruptive force within nationalism which, if given free reign after 1815, would have rapidly destroyed the peace settlement. Another approach by modern historians has been to question the assumptions of earlier generations that support for liberalism and nationalism was widespread in early nineteenth-century Europe. The present historical consensus is that the liberal nationalism of the early nineteenth century was largely a middle class affair. Among the masses, the nationalistic feeling aroused during the Napoleonic Wars was primarily a primitive anti-foreigner nationalism, expressing resentment at French fiscal exactions, depredations and occupation. The logical conclusion to be drawn from this approach is that the Vienna statesmen cannot be criticised for ignoring the (alleged) national aspirations of the masses, which scarcely existed in 1815.

The proposition that the smaller powers would have exercised a beneficial influence over the outcome of the peace settlement, if allowed to participate more fully, is problematic. Historically, there is no evidence that smaller powers behave less selfishly than Great Powers. What is certain is that if Holland and some of the German states (as well as Prussia) had dictated the terms of the Second Treaty of Paris in November 1815, France would have been dismembered.

The assertion that the Vienna statesmen were a motley collection of 'museum pieces', arch reactionaries out of touch with the spirit of the age, has also been questioned by modern historians. They are now seen as a not untypical sample of European royalty and aristocracy, men whose formative years had been influenced by the Enlightenment (the essentially rationalist and largely anti-religious philosophical movement of the eighteenth century) only to see these noble ideals betrayed by the 'bloody tyranny' of the French Revolution. Furthermore, the Revolution was followed by continual warfare, prolonged by the ambitions of Napoleon's dictatorship. In short, they were disillusioned men. As a consequence, the Vienna system was based on negative premises – it was a rejection of hegemony by one power, of war and of revolution. The settlement was therefore necessarily concerned with re-establishing order within states as well as order between states. Although it failed in respect of internal order, as shown by the revolutions of the next decades, it succeeded in preserving peace between the Great Powers for at least 40 years. This is one important reason why, since 1914, historians have been much less critical of the work of the peacemakers in 1814–15.

The settlement that followed the Napoleonic Wars has, in general, benefited rather than suffered from comparison with the peace treaties which followed the First and Second World Wars. The Versailles Treaty of 1919, dubbed 'the twenty years' truce', clearly lacked the durability of the Vienna Treaty, which ushered in a century free from conflicts involving all the Great Powers. Nor did the statesmen of 1814–15 commit the major error of enforcing a dictated peace on the defeated nation, like the '*diktat* of Versailles', which created a legacy of deeply felt resentment that undermined European stability for two decades. The Vienna statesmen could even be credited with having experimented with international cooperation in peacetime, in the form of the Congress System. After 1945, some west European observers began to fear that the Second World War had destroyed the Nazi tyranny only to see another (Stalinist) one imposed over eastern Europe. In 1815, on the other hand, Castlereagh and Metternich fought very hard to prevent the hegemony of Russia replacing that of France. It might be said of the Vienna Settlement, therefore, that 'distance lends enchantment to the view'.

* Modern historians (French excepted) tend, therefore, to focus on the merits of the 1815 settlement, in that Europe enjoyed 40 years of peace until the Crimean War and a century without a major conflict.

This may not, of course, have been wholly due to the nature of the peace treaties themselves. For example, the fear that war amongst the Great Powers would encourage the revolutionary forces that supposedly lurked in the back streets of European cities was a powerful inducement to maintain peace. But it seems clear that the stability of the new European states system owed much to the statesmanlike treatment of France in both 1814 and 1815, which Castlereagh, above all, strongly advocated. France's leaders and most French historians, however, were not so impressed at the allies' generosity towards the defeated nation. They came to realise that the barriers erected against French expansion denied her the ability to exercise the sort of influence over her immediate neighbours (Belgium and Italy) that was normal for a Great Power. They also resented the existence of the 'Waterloo League', the Quadruple Alliance of 1815, which seemed to place France in a state of 'quarantine' as a purveyor of contagious political diseases unwelcome to other states. Nevertheless, France was re-admitted to the Great Powers' club in 1818, so her grievances were not that serious, even if her pride remained hurt.

The attempt to re-establish a balance of power has also been viewed with favour by modern historians since it seems probable that a major factor for peace was that none of the Great Powers had a genuine reason to feel aggrieved at the peace terms, which satisfied most of their territorial claims. This is the sense in which an American writer suggests that the new international order was 'legitimized' in the eyes of the Great Powers. It produced stability because all were willing to try to resolve problems that arose within the new framework, created in 1815, rather than attempt to destroy it in order to achieve their individual ambitions. Nevertheless, the balance arrived at was not really workable in central Europe. The main weakness was that Austria's financial and military resources were not adequate for her new role as defender of the status quo against challenges from France in the west and Russia in the east.

In conclusion, from the perspective of the present, the Vienna Settlement has much more to commend it than most contemporary commentators and later historians allowed. Much of this favourable reappraisal stems from the disillusioning experience of more recent peace settlements, particularly perhaps the de-stabilising effects of the principle of 'self-determination' after 1919. Some of it also derives from the publication in recent years of detailed studies of the main partici-pants at the peace conference that present them in a more sympathetic and favourable light than the old caricature of the Vienna statesmen as a clique of reactionary freaks. That – from the point of view of the educated middle classes of Europe – they were too obsessed with the recent past and too little endowed with vision for the future may be fair comment. Viewed as a Great Power settlement, on the other hand, it

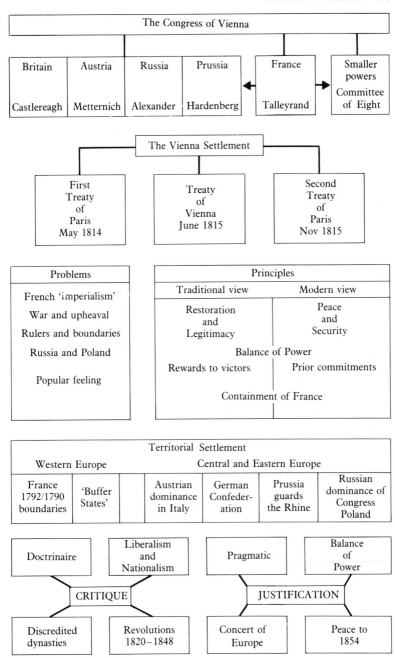

The Congress of Vienna

Britain	Austria	Russia	Prussia	France	Smaller powers Committee of Eight
Castlereagh	Metternich	Alexander	Hardenberg	Talleyrand	

The Vienna Settlement

First Treaty of Paris May 1814	Treaty of Vienna June 1815	Second Treaty of Paris Nov 1815

Problems	Principles	
French 'imperialism'	Traditional view	Modern view
War and upheaval	Restoration and Legitimacy	Peace and Security
Rulers and boundaries		
Russia and Poland	Balance of Power	
Popular feeling	Rewards to victors	Prior commitments
	Containment of France	

Territorial Settlement

Western Europe			Central and Eastern Europe			
France 1792/1790 boundaries	'Buffer States'		Austrian dominance in Italy	German Confederation	Prussia guards the Rhine	Russian dominance of Congress Poland

Doctrinaire	Liberalism and Nationalism	Pragmatic	Balance of Power
	CRITIQUE	JUSTIFICATION	
Discredited dynasties	Revolutions 1820–1848	Concert of Europe	Peace to 1854

Summary – The Congress of Vienna

was pragmatic, not doctrinaire, and a reasonable compromise between the interests of the leading states.

Whether it was possible to satisfy aspirations for more freedom and national unity while creating a stable international system after 20 years of war is not immediately obvious. On reflection, it would appear that a peace settlement which satisfied popular demands for freedom and nationhood would have been very different from the one made in 1814–15. A radically different peace treaty, however, would almost certainly have left one or more of the Great Powers dissatisfied, and so have undermined the stability of the international order created in 1815. It looks to be a case, therefore, of a choice – between freedom and national independence or peace and stability.

Making notes on 'The Congress of Vienna'

The notes you make on this chapter will need to be a record that you can refer to when you are revising. You will need to know both the main facts about the peace settlement *and* the issues that historians have considered to be important. Use the summary diagram on page 33 as the framework for your notes, which will, therefore, be divided into seven sections – although you may find it more convenient to combine sections 6 and 7.

1. The Congress of Vienna. List those taking part (the states and their representatives) and identify their major interests.
2. The Vienna Settlement. What were the three parts? Why were there three parts?
3. Problems. Explain the five major problems facing the peacemakers.
4. Principles. What principles have been identified as underpinning the settlement? In each case decide how valid the identification is.
5. Territorial Settlement. Study the maps on pages 18 and 25. Using the six sub-headings in the diagram, list the distribution of territory made by the peacemakers. Make sure that you know where each place is.
6. Critique. What criticisms have been made of the peace settlement? In each case say whether you think the criticism is justified.
7. Justification. What arguments have been put forward in defence of the peace settlement? Are they convincing?

Answering essay questions on 'The Congress of Vienna'

The Congress of Vienna is one of the most popular topics among examiners of nineteenth-century European History, if one is to judge by the number of questions that have been set in the past. It is, therefore, a topic well worth preparing thoroughly. Questions tend to require you to make an assessment of the Vienna Settlement, especially in terms of one of the following: the aims of the peacemakers and the extent to which their aims were achieved; the effects of the settlement; its success or failure.

The most straightforward types of question are directly phrased, such as:

1. 'What were the aims of the peacemakers at Vienna? How far were they achieved?'
2. 'How far did the Vienna Settlement restore the stability of Europe that Napoleon had destroyed?'
3. 'Was the Vienna Settlement a success?'

With 'double' questions such as question 1, you have a choice. You can either tackle the questions separately, one after the other, or you can select a number of aspects of the topic as paragraph points, and deal with both questions in each main paragraph. The second option is often to be preferred because it results in a more unified essay. If you choose this approach, include an overview answer to the first question as an introduction. What would you include in the concluding paragraph? An acceptable answer to these questions could be constructed around a series of paragraph points such as 'balance of power', where you assume that the peacemakers did have coherent aims. A higher quality answer would draw attention to the disputes among historians and would qualify statements of aims so as to show that historical uncertainties exist. If you adopted the second approach, what paragraph points other than 'balance of power' would you select?

Essay questions on the Vienna Settlement are very often of the 'challenging statement' type, however, in which you are provided with a quotation and are asked to discuss it. Look at the following seven examples of this type of question.

4. '"The Congress of Vienna solved every problem except the ones that mattered." Discuss.'
5. 'Discuss the view that "The Congress of Vienna created more problems than it solved".'
6. 'Is it valid to assert that "much of the Vienna Settlement was sensible and just, and not vindictive"?'
7. '"The Congress of Vienna was doomed to failure where it attempted to wipe out the effects of the last quarter century of European history." Discuss.'
8. '"Concern for the restoration and maintenance of legitimate rulers dominated the decisions made at the Congress of Vienna." Discuss.'
9. '"The arrangements made at the Congress of Vienna were right in principle but wrong in detail." Do you agree?'

10. '"After the Napoleonic Wars France was still regarded as the greatest threat to peace in Europe." Do the terms of the Vienna Settlement support this view?'

Your first task when confronted with a 'challenging statement' question is consciously to identify the *aspect* of the topic (in question form) you are being asked to consider. Do this with the seven examples above. You should spot, for example, that question 8 is asking 'What were the aims of the peacemakers?' Most examination questions of this type offer you one of the possible answers that could be given to the historical question concerned. Your second task is the straightforward one of identifying the answer that the quotation supplies. For example, in question 8 you are offered 'the restoration and maintenance of legitimate rulers' as the aim of the peacemakers. Rarely is the point of view expressed in the quotation more than a partial answer to the historical question. Your third task is to identify the other possible answers that should be considered. You should already have done this for question 8 when you worked on question 1, above. Select another question (question 7 might be the most suitable) and carry out the second and third tasks on it.

Further stages of dealing with 'challenging statement' questions will be discussed on pages 57 and 100.

Source-based questions on 'The Congress of Vienna'

1 Success or failure?
Study the three verdicts on the Congress given on pages 28–30. Answer the following questions.
a) Are the three writers generally supportive or generally critical of the peace settlement? (1 mark)
b) The first and third extracts criticise the settlement on the basis of what it lacked. What similarities are there between these criticisms? (5 marks)
c) What does the author of the second extract suggest the treaties were based on? (2 marks)
d) What can be deduced about the values and attitudes of the three authors from the criticisms they make? What values and attitudes do they hold in common? (7 marks)

CHAPTER 3

The Congress System

1 Introduction

The Congress System, which took the form of a series of congresses held between 1818 and 1822, can be regarded as a practical expression of the rather general concept of the Concert of Europe. The Concert itself was little more than an ideal – an attempt to harmonise the conflicting ambitions of the Great Powers in the interests of 'Europe' as a whole. As such, its effectiveness was dependent on the willingness of all five Great Powers to show restraint in the pursuit of their individual interests. Without this it would be almost impossible to reach a consensus on important issues. Although the Concert was an abstract concept, lacking a precise mode of operation, it would be rash to dismiss it as a mere will-o'-the wisp. True, it was described as a 'phantasm' by an English minister in the 1880s, but by then the Concert had been in decline for nearly 30 years. In 1840, by contrast, the French premier asserted his belief in 'the necessity of the Concert among the Great Powers on important questions'. The translation into practice of the ideal of diplomatic cooperation for the sake of European peace and stability could take more than one form. The first attempt at it was the Congress System.

The four congresses held at Aix-la-Chapelle, Troppau, Laibach and Verona were an attempt to prolong into the post-war period the Great Power alliance which had maintained a sense of common purpose in the final stages of the war against Napoleon. This sense of common purpose derived from the almost unique continuing personal contact between the statesmen of the period. For example, both Alexander and Castlereagh spent well over a year away from 'home' between 1813 and 1815, attending a series of meetings and conferences to coordinate allied policy towards France. It was this experience which convinced Castlereagh of the benefits to be expected from 'the habits of confidential intercourse which a long residence with the principal actors has established'. It is not surprising, therefore, that the desire to carry on consulting together took the form of congresses attended by the same familiar figures. When the problem arose in 1818 of how to satisfy France's claim as a Great Power to participate in these consultations, it was solved by an agreement to admit her to future congresses. However, this apparently straightforward solution tends to obscure the fact that both France and Russia had wanted to enlarge the membership and extend the scope of diplomatic gatherings.

In one sense, therefore, the Congress System was a sort of straightjacket imposed on the restless ambitions of France and Russia by Castlereagh and Metternich. Furthermore, although the phrase 'Congress System' is a convenient term for describing these meetings of the representatives of the five Great Powers, it can also be misleading. For one thing, there was no real 'system' behind this series of meetings, which were arranged on an *ad hoc* basis and conducted without any rules of procedure. To add to the confusion, congresses were not the only form of diplomatic gathering that took place after 1815. Conferences of ambassadors were also held, but these generally only considered one specific topic whereas a congress usually discussed a number of matters of common concern to the Great Powers. Another distinction between the two types of meetings was that monarchs and foreign ministers often attended congresses, which gave them a more exalted status than an ambassadorial conference.

A congress took place because all the Great Powers agreed to hold such a meeting. If they did not, a conference might be held instead – for example the Hanover meeting between Castlereagh and Metternich in October 1821. In fact, Metternich was rather reluctant to agree to a congress if he thought he could manipulate an ambassadorial conference more easily at Vienna, where the resident ambassadors were sarcastically dubbed his 'harem'. Another complication was that the Congress System did not operate in a diplomatic vacuum. Once the common purpose of the Alliance had been fulfilled in the defeat of France in 1815, international relations resumed their normal course. In other words, mutual suspicion, competition and rivalry were once again the order of the day as sovereign states set about the pursuit of their national interests. However, the rivalry between states was lessened by informal understandings between some of the Great Powers. From 1815 to 1820, for example, Austria and Britain worked closely together to contain France and to control Russia. When this informal cooperation broke down over disagreements about the purpose of the Alliance, Austria was able to enlist Russia's support (in addition to Prussia's) for a policy of resistance to revolution in Europe.

The main obstacle to the successful working of the Congress System turned out to be that a consensus did not necessarily exist on the fundamental question of the purpose of the alliance of the Great Powers in peacetime. Although the issues to be discussed at a congress were certainly matters of common concern, it did not follow that all would agree on what action was appropriate to a particular situation. This problem was not apparent immediately after 1815, since the victor powers shared a common interest in the treatment of France. In 1820, however, it became acute when the Great Powers met to consider what to do about revolts in some of the smaller states. By this time Metternich was attempting to dominate the management of the congresses, even though Castlereagh had been the main architect of the Congress System.

2 Origins of the Congress System

It seemed to Castlereagh that the experience of successful cooperation in the Fourth Coalition against France from 1813 to 1814 gave reason to believe that renewal of this personal contact could help to keep the peace and provide for security in the future. Accordingly, he secured acceptance of a clause to this effect in the Treaty of Chaumont (March 1814) in the form of Article V, which read:

1 The High Contracting Parties, reserving to themselves to concert together, on the conclusion of a Peace with France as to the means best adapted to guarantee to Europe, and to themselves reciprocally, the continuance of the Peace, have also determined to enter
5 without delay, into defensive engagements for the Protection of their respective States in Europe against every attempt which France might make to infringe the order of things resulting from such Pacification.

The Treaty of Chaumont, however, was rather too exclusively an alliance directed against France to serve as a basis for a general forum discussing matters of common concern to the Great Powers. In Article VI of the Quadruple Alliance (November 1815) the idea of periodic meetings serving a wider purpose was proposed:

1 To facilitate and to secure the execution of the present Treaty, and to consolidate the connections which at the present moment so closely unite the Four Sovereigns for the happiness of the world . . . the High Contracting Parties have agreed to renew
5 their meeting at fixed periods . . . for the purpose of consulting upon their common interests, and for the consideration of the measures which at each of these periods shall be considered the most salutary for the repose and prosperity of Nations, and for the maintenance of the peace of Europe.

But in Tsar Alexander's view, this was too mundane a basis for an alliance, which ought to rest on 'the sublime truths which the Holy Religion of our Saviour teaches'. In September 1815, he had persuaded Prussia and Austria (the latter with some scepticism) to conclude the treaty known as the Holy Alliance, which proclaimed:

1 . . . their fixed resolution, both in the administration of their respective States and in their political relations with every other Government, to take for their sole guide the precepts of that Holy Religion, namely, the precepts of Justice, Christian Charity and
5 Peace, which . . . must have an immediate influence on the councils of Princes, and guide all their steps, as being the only

means of consolidating human institutions and remedying their imperfections. In consequence their Majesties have agreed on the following Articles:

10 *Art I.* Conformably to the words of the Holy Scriptures, the Three Contracting Monarchs will remain united by the bonds of a true and indissoluble fraternity, and considering each other as fellow countrymen, they will . . . lend each other aid and assistance; and, regarding themselves towards their subjects and

15 armies as fathers of families, they will lead them, in the same spirit of fraternity with which they are animated, to protect Religion, Peace, and Justice.

Art II. In consequence, the sole principle of force, whether between the said Governments or between their Subjects, shall be

20 that of doing each other reciprocal service, and of testifying by unalterable goodwill the mutual affection with which they ought to be animated, to consider themselves all as members of one and the same Christian nation . . .

It is not very surprising that the Holy Alliance should be dubbed 'a piece of sublime mysticism and nonsense' by the Tsar's contemporaries. In view of Alexander's notorious oscillation of moods, it would be easy to dismiss the Holy Alliance as just the manifestation of a passing fit of religious mania. But there was possibly more to it than that. About ten years earlier Alexander had expressed similar sentiments to the British government and had suggested the creation of a new league, based on a revised law of nations. The British reply, in January 1805, had stressed the need for a defensive pact to check what it called 'projects of aggrandizement and ambition similar to those which have produced all the calamities inflicted on Europe since the disastrous era of the French Revolution'.

* The views expressed in these Anglo-Russian proposals of 1804–5 could be regarded as providing some of the inspiration behind the Congress System. What is lacking in these early exchanges is the experience of successful collaboration in a succession of meetings and conferences, which was gained in the period 1813–15. The origins of the Congress System, therefore, do lie primarily in the Quadruple Alliance of 1815, overlaid by Alexander's somewhat bizarre scheme of the Holy Alliance. The effect of the latter was to create some ambiguity at the outset regarding the purpose and the scope of the post-war Alliance of the Great Powers. It was therefore uncertain whether the Congress System was authorised to act in the name of Europe on the basis of the Treaty of Vienna and the Quadruple Alliance of 1815 or on the basis of the high sounding moral principles enunciated in the Holy Alliance. This uncertainty was to create major difficulties for the working of the Congress System.

3 The Congresses

a) The Congress of Aix-la-Chapelle, September–November 1818

The Congress of Aix-la-Chapelle was convened in September 1818 to consider matters relating to France. It was attended by the rulers of Russia, Austria and Prussia as well as the leading ministers of the four Great Powers. It was agreed without much difficulty to end the partial military occupation of France by allied forces which had been a source of bitterness and a cause of instability in French politics since 1815. The question of France's position in the Concert of Europe was more controversial. The Tsar pressed the case for transforming the Quadruple Alliance into a five-power alliance by the inclusion of France. Ostensibly this was on the grounds of monarchical solidarity, allowing the Bourbon monarchy in France to take its place as another bastion of order against possible unrest in Europe. In reality, his aim was to facilitate a Franco-Russian alignment directed against Britain and Austria. Castlereagh and Metternich therefore opposed the Russian plan, offering a compromise solution instead. France would be admitted to the Congress System, under Article VI of the treaty of November 1815, but the allies would also renew their commitments to each other against France, under the Treaty of Chaumont of 1814.

Although the Tsar accepted this compromise proposal, he was not really satisfied with it, since he had hoped to persuade the Congress to agree to his latest pet project – a scheme for an *Alliance Solidaire* (Universal Union). This general alliance, open to all the signatories of the Vienna Treaty, would guarantee to all sovereigns their thrones and territorial possessions, which was supposed to encourage them to grant constitutions to their subjects. Castlereagh poured cold water on Alexander's 'Empire of Christian morality', persuading the Tsar that the British government could not take on commitments over and above its existing treaty obligations.

The Congress of Aix-la-Chapelle was a successful demonstration of Anglo-Austrian cooperation, but French hopes of a *rapprochement* with Russia did not materialise. This was partly as a result of Metternich's skill, in private talks, in sowing mutual mistrust between them. The main business of the Congress, to determine France's relationship with the other powers, was concluded quite harmoniously, but on minor issues, such as the slave trade and the Spanish colonies, acrimonious exchanges took place between Britain and France. However, the most serious aspect of the meeting was the Tsar's attempt to change the existing alliance into a territorial guarantee of all the states which had participated in the Congress of Vienna.

b) The Congress of Troppau, October–December 1820

In the interval between the ending of the first congress in 1818 and the summoning of the second at Troppau in October 1820, Metternich's warnings of the existence of a European revolutionary conspiracy seemed well justified. Liberal unrest in Germany (which had been suppressed) was followed in 1820 by the assassination of the Duc de Berry, the heir-apparent to the French throne, and by revolutions in Spain, Portugal and Naples.

The Great Powers showed most concern at the Spanish and Neapolitan revolts. Although the demand for a constitution in Portugal alarmed the conservative powers, they confined themselves to making formal protests to the government at Lisbon. This was a tacit recognition of the fact that Portugal enjoyed British 'protection', as shown by the presence of a naval squadron in the river Tagus which could dominate the capital.

Although the revolts of the early 1820s in the smaller states followed a common pattern, there is absolutely no evidence of a central committee in Paris directing these revolutionary outbreaks, as Metternich alleged. The revolts were caused by general discontent with arbitrary and incompetent government and with the restoration of clerical and aristocratic privileges. The impetus to revolt came from within the ranks of the army. The revolts either began with a mutiny or took the form of a military *coup*. Many army officers at this period held liberal views and had grievances over being poorly and irregularly paid. Discontented army officers found natural allies among the progressive urban middle class and some of the lesser nobility. Links between them existed through membership of secret societies, such as the *Carbonari* in Naples.

The main demand of the revolutionaries was for a constitution. The Neapolitans adopted the Spanish constitution of 1812 as their model, even though it was regarded by many liberals in western Europe as seriously flawed. In the first place, it allowed the monarch so little real power that no self-respecting ruler would willingly tolerate it. Secondly, it denied the ministers enough control over the assembly to provide effective government and political stability. The refusal of the Spanish and Neapolitan revolutionaries to accept advice to modify their constitutions not only alienated conservative elements within the state but also lessened French and British sympathy for them.

The revolution in Spain, which began with an army revolt at Cadiz in January 1820, was a protest against despotic rule. On his return to Spain in 1814, Ferdinand VII had rapidly restored all the former privileges of the aristocracy and Church. He had also revoked the 1812 constitution and proceeded to rule in a ruthless and arbitrary manner, exiling or imprisoning many liberals.

The Neapolitan revolt which began in July 1820 had many features in common with that of Spain, but there was a more genuinely popular base to the revolutionary movement there. A constitutional chamber was summoned and a constitution was created, to which the King took an oath of loyalty, albeit reluctantly. The rebels' refusal to seek a workable compromise with the King inevitably increased the danger of intervention by one of the Great Powers.

* The revolutions in Spain and Naples presented Metternich with a major test of statesmanship. It was clear that a consensus was impossible to achieve over Spain. The Tsar was pressing for 'authorised intervention' by the Alliance. This might take the form of a French military occupation of Spain or, failing that, the despatch of a Russian army to restore Ferdinand as an absolute monarch. Metternich disliked both of these alternatives. The first might result in Spain falling under French influence, while the prospect of a Russian army marching across Europe was little short of a nightmare. Metternich's objections were supported by Castlereagh, who insisted that the Quadruple Alliance had not been designed to suppress revolutions. 'The Alliance was made against France', he said, and argued that the situation in Spain did not justify intervention.

Metternich's solution to the problem of Spain was to persuade the Tsar that the Spanish situation was not urgent enough to require immediate consideration by the Great Powers, suggesting that the revolt in Madrid would burn itself out. More to the point, events in Spain were not a direct threat to Austrian interests whereas the revolt in Naples might lead to unrest in other parts of Italy.

Metternich wanted to secure an outright condemnation of the Neapolitan revolt by all the powers. He also insisted on securing the moral backing of the Alliance for Austrian military intervention, in part because he may have feared that once her forces were engaged in Italy, Austria was vulnerable to Russian pressure along her northern borders. Consequently, when the Tsar supported France's demand for a congress on Naples in August 1820, Metternich was faced with a possible Franco-Russian front. He was rightly suspicious of the French initiative for a congress. Their aim was to use collective intervention by the Alliance to press the Neapolitans into adopting a system of government modelled on the French Charter of 1814. If successful, this would have made France stand out as the patron of constitutional government in Italy and as a rival focus of influence to Austria with the Italian states.

When the Tsar arrived at Troppau in September 1820, accompanied by his liberal-minded adviser, Capodistrias, he was still wavering and undecided as to whether he would support France or Austria at the Congress. On the one hand, he shared Metternich's alarm at the challenge to monarchical authority posed by the revolutions, supposedly inspired by French ideals and organised in France. But, at the same time, he believed that political discontent should be lessened by institutional reforms to promote good government. An additional consideration was the tactical advantage to be gained by siding with Austria in the hope of destroying the Anglo-Austrian *entente* which had existed since 1815. Alexander therefore brought to the Congress two different proposals. One proclaimed the right of the Alliance to intervene to put down revolts, while the second proposed that the smaller states should be allowed to introduce reforms with the consent of the Great Powers. Clearly, the first would drive a wedge between Britain and Austria, while the second would antagonise Metternich, but please France.

The French representatives at Troppau had been instructed by their government to obtain Russia's cooperation against Austria for the creation of a moderate constitutional regime in Naples. This was a very ambitious scheme, requiring considerable diplomatic skill to outwit Metternich, and with no backing from Britain. Castlereagh had made Britain's position clear before the Congress met. This was completely at variance with the French stance, in that it opposed intervention by the Great Powers collectively, while conceding Austria's right to act under the terms of the Austro-Neapolitan Treaty of 1815, in order to maintain her influence over Italy. 'The revolution in Naples', Castlereagh argued, 'should be treated as a special rather than as a general question, as an Italian question rather than as a European, and consequently as in the sphere of Austria rather than of the Alliance'.

* The fact that both Britain and France only sent observers to the Congress, who only attended the formal sessions, made it easier for Metternich to hold private talks with the Tsar. At nightly tea-drinking sessions with Alexander, he was able to work on the Tsar's fears of revolution, with a remarkable array of documentary 'proofs' of the sinister activities of secret societies. Since Metternich now gave priority to the battle against revolution, he was prepared to abandon his former policy of cooperation with Britain for the sake of a closer relationship with Russia. Alexander, for his part, was willing to be persuaded that all Europe was threatened by revolutionary conspiracies, directed from Paris, and that he must abandon his liberal inclinations and support Austria in a policy of suppressing any revolution. Prussia, which had virtually given up an independent foreign policy since the outbreak of unrest in the German states in 1818, readily fell into line behind Austria. The outcome was the Troppau Protocol, signed by the three eastern powers in November 1820, despite the protests of the British and French observers. The Protocol was uncompromising in its assertion that intervention in the name of the Alliance was justified if revolutions occurred:

1 States which have undergone a change of Government due to revolution, the results of which threaten other states, *ipso facto* cease to be members of the European Alliance, and remain excluded from it until their situation gives guarantees for legal

5 order and stability. If, owing to such situations, immediate danger threatens other states, the Powers bind themselves, by peaceful means, or if need be by arms, to bring back the guilty state into the bosom of the Great Alliance.

The Troppau Protocol established the principle of a united front of the three eastern powers against the forces of revolution, which lasted for nearly 30 years. The objections of Britain and France to it seemed to surprise them, as shown in this Circular of December 1820 to the embassies abroad of the three eastern powers:

1 There is nothing new in the system followed by Austria, Prussia and Russia; it rests upon the same maxims as those which served as bases of the Treaties upon which the Alliance of the European States was founded. They only wish to maintain Peace, and to
5 deliver Europe from the curse of Revolution, and to remove or abridge, as much as in them lies, the evils which result from the violation of all principles of order and morality.

In the hope of persuading the western powers to accept the Troppau Protocol it was agreed not to publish it until after the Congress had resumed at Laibach, in January 1821.

c) The Congress of Laibach, January–May 1821

The main purpose of the Congress of Laibach was supposedly to attempt some sort of mediation by the Great Powers between King Ferdinand of Naples and his subjects. However, at the Congress there was little attempt at any serious mediation. The new regime had rejected France's advice to modify the constitution along the lines of the French 'Charter' of 1814. The Tsar's attitude towards the revolution had also hardened after the outbreak of a mutiny at St Petersburg in December 1820. Consequently, the Congress gave Austria a mandate to intervene by force, which resulted in the defeat of the Neapolitan army by Austrian troops in March 1821 and the overthrow of the revolutionary regime.

A rising in Piedmont in March 1821 was also suppressed by Austrian troops with the blessing of the Congress, the Tsar even offering to put 100,000 men at Austria's disposal. With an Austrian military presence established in Tuscany and the Papal States, the whole of Italy was placed under Austrian military surveillance. Before the Laibach Congress broke up, news arrived of the outbreak in April 1821 of a revolt in Greece against the rule of the Sultan of Turkey. This seemed to confirm Metternich's view that revolution, inspired from France, was rampant. To the Tsar he said, 'It is at Paris that the great furnace exists . . . for the most vast conspiracy that has ever threatened the whole of society'.

The Congress of Laibach was a complete triumph for Metternich. France's attempt to support the cause of moderate revolution had been a failure, serving only to annoy the Tsar. Alexander had been persuaded to abandon the cause of liberalism and to seek safety in the precepts of the Troppau Protocol. Although the Tsar was later to become very restless at the turn of events in Greece, it was agreed in May 1821 that the Sultan of Turkey should be assured that the Great Powers would not give aid to the rebellious Greeks. Metternich's policy of opposing all revolutions had therefore succeeded. The only set-back was Britain's open condemnation of interference in the domestic affairs of other states in the name of the Alliance. Despite the apparent decline of the Anglo-Austrian *entente*, however, which had operated effectively from 1815 to 1820 as a check on France and Russia, there was still some common ground between Britain and Austria on some issues, especially in the Near East.

d) The Congress of Verona, October–December 1822

Between the ending of the Laibach Congress in May 1821 and the start of the Congress of Verona in October 1822, the dominant issues in international affairs were the Greek revolt and the continuing problem of Spain. Once the Tsar had returned to Russia in May 1821, Metternich feared that he could not be relied upon to abstain indefinitely from intervening in the Greek revolt.

Russia had two grounds for action against the Turks. Not only were the Greeks members of the Orthodox religion, over which Russia had some shadowy claims to be regarded as the guardian, but she also had grievances against Turkey over the non-fulfilment of the Treaty of Bucharest of 1812. In the summer of 1821, the Tsar veered from one course to another. In July, he hinted to France that the time was ripe for an alliance but by August he was expressing his fears of revolution by saying 'If we reply to the Turks with war, the Committee in Paris will triumph and no government will be left on its feet'. By the summer of 1822, the Tsar had resigned himself to await the decision of the Conference, arranged for September in Vienna, as a preliminary meeting before the full Congress at Verona.

In the event, the Greek problem was not a very contentious issue at either meeting. Collective diplomatic pressure on the Sultan applied by the Great Powers secured satisfaction for Russia's grievances against the Turks, while Metternich once more succeeded in persuading the Tsar that the Greek revolt was but a part of an international revolutionary conspiracy.

The dominant issue at Verona turned out to be the Tsar's insistence that the Troppau Protocol should be applied to Spain. Although his plan for intervention by an allied army was rejected by Austria, France and Britain, he remained adamant that the only aim of the Alliance was 'to combat Revolution'. Since he had agreed not to destroy the unity of the Alliance by siding with the Greek insurgents, he demanded that the Alliance now prove its worth by responding to the Spanish King's appeals to the Great Powers to suppress the revolution.

While the British were, as usual, opposed to any interference in the domestic affairs of another state, the French were undecided about what to do. But they had at least resolved that if a French army did enter Spain, it would not be as an agent of the Alliance, but as a demonstration that France could act independently. This divergence of view put Metternich in a quandary. He did not want to give Russia an excuse for marching an army across Europe but he feared that a French army might set up a constitutional monarchy in Spain, which would set a 'bad example' to the Italian states. Any intervention in the name of the Alliance would alienate Britain, whose support Austria needed to keep Russia in check in the Near East. Metternich's solution to this dilemma was to persuade France to join the other three powers in sending Protest Notes simultaneously to Madrid. The Notes would be couched in such threatening terms that the Spanish government would be obliged to react, possibly in such a way that would justify allied intervention.

This scheme enabled Metternich to preserve an appearance of moral solidarity among the four powers. It also went sufficiently far towards satisfying the Tsar's demand for action against the revolution in Spain to enable Metternich to persuade him to maintain a united front towards the Greek revolt. Much to Metternich's satisfaction, therefore, the Congress of Verona concluded with a general condemnation of the Greek revolt as 'a rash and criminal enterprise'.

4 The Breakdown of the Congress System

The Congress System broke down in 1823 under the weight of the discordance among the Great Powers in their attitudes towards revolutions. In defiance of the policy agreed at Verona, France intervened in Spain in 1823 to suppress the revolt, while in 1827 Russia, backed by Britain and France, defied the spirit of the Troppau Protocol to assist the Greek revolt. Although it was France and Russia who openly rejected Metternich's tutelage, it was nevertheless Britain's attitude that was most responsible for the collapse of the Congress System. Castlereagh's personal commitment to the Alliance tended to conceal the growing restiveness of British public opinion over involvement in continental affairs. His successor, Canning, openly repudiated the whole concept of congress diplomacy in 1823. Verona was therefore the last of the congresses.

Metternich's satisfaction at having achieved a solution of the Spanish problem at the Congress of Verona was shortlived. With the appointment of Chateaubriand as the new Foreign Minister in France in 1823,

French policy became more decisive. 'Our true policy', he declared, 'is the Russian policy, by which we counterbalance two declared enemies: Austria and England' – language hardly consonant with the spirit of the Alliance. France did not abide by the agreement to deliver a severe Diplomatic Note to Madrid simultaneously with the three eastern powers. Instead, a French army of 100,000 men marched into Spain in April 1823, and restored the authority of the Spanish King. The French invasion of Spain without a mandate from the Alliance was an assertion of France's right to pursue an independent foreign policy. The French Prime Minister had made this clear to Wellington before the Congress of Verona, in saying that 'French policy in relation to Spain was founded upon French interests, and . . . entirely unconnected with anything the congress might determine.'

This unilateral military action, although approved by the Tsar, had not been sanctioned by the Alliance. Metternich, in fact, made a desperate attempt to persuade the other Great Powers to join Austria in stopping it, but to no avail. Canning, who took over the Foreign Office on Castlereagh's death in August 1822, disapproved of the French invasion of Spain, but he would not cooperate with Metternich to oppose it. He could at least take consolation from the fact that France's action had not been given a European mandate at Verona, thereby demonstrating the disunity of the Alliance. The 'Congress System' was clearly in ruins in the spring of 1823, given the disarray among the Great Powers over such an important issue.

The divergence of views among the five Great Powers became even more explicit a few years later, in the course of the Greek revolt. In 1827 Britain and France agreed to cooperate with Russia in assisting a rebellion against a legitimate authority, in defiance of Austrian and Prussian insistence on respect for the rights of the Sultan of Turkey over the Greeks.

* However, the breakdown of the Congress System had been inevitable since 1820 because the views of Britain, and possibly France, towards revolutions in minor states were incompatible with the attitude of the three eastern powers. The revolts of 1820 raised the fundamental question of the purpose of the Alliance of the Great Powers. Metternich insisted on a general right of intervention by the Alliance, enshrined in the Troppau Protocol, accepted by Russia and Prussia, but rejected by both France and Britain. Its acceptance by the Tsar marked the end of Russian liberalism, and signified that Alexander had finally been persuaded of the 'reality' of Metternich's mythical universal revolutionary conspiracy, based in Paris. Castlereagh, who was prepared to concede Austria's right to intervene in Naples, forcefully repudiated Metternich's interpretation of the purpose of the Alliance as providing a justification for interference in the domestic affairs of other states, regardless of whether the security of the Great Powers was at risk. Hence his refusal to associate Britain with 'the moral responsibility of

administering a general European police'. Castlereagh also complained to the French, in September 1820, that the Tsar was trying to turn the Alliance of the five Great Powers into a general government of Europe, despite the fact that the terms of the Alliance had been fixed in 1815 and 1818. 'To apply them to all revolutionary events', he said, 'is to pervert the principle. It is the Holy Alliance as conceived by the Tsar and which we cannot adopt'.

The attitude of the Cabinet and public opinion in Britain also contributed to the breakdown of the Congress System. During the Congress of Aix-la-Chapelle Castlereagh was warned by the Cabinet not to agree to any extension of Britain's commitments to the Alliance, whose purpose, in peacetime, was not well understood by an insular nation. It was therefore quite clear to Castlereagh by 1820, if not earlier, that British opinion was reluctant to accept the need for the continuance of Britain's participation in continental affairs, when no danger existed to the security of the Great Powers. In his State Paper of May 1820, Castlereagh explained his own misgivings about intervention by the Alliance in the affairs of other states such as Spain.

1 In this Alliance, nothing is more likely to impair, or even destroy
   its real utility, than any attempt to push its duties and its
   obligations beyond the Sphere which its original conception and
   understood Principles will warrant. It was an Union for the
5 re-conquest and liberation of a great proportion of the Continent
   of Europe from the military dominion of France; and having
   subdued the Conqueror, it took the State of Possession, as
   established by the Peace, under the protection of the Alliance. It
   never was, however, intended as an Union for the Government of
10 the World, or for the Superintendence of the Internal Affairs of
   other States.
     It provided specifically against an infraction on the part of
   France of the state of possession then created ... It further
   designated the Revolutionary Power which had convulsed France
15 and desolated Europe, as an object of its constant solicitude, but
   it was the Revolutionary power more particularly in its Military
   Character actual and existent within France against which it
   intended to take precautions, rather than against the Democratic
   Principles, then as now, but too generally spread throughout
20 Europe ...
    ... The principle of one state interfering by force in the internal
   affairs of another, in order to enforce obedience to the governing
   authority, is always a question of the greatest possible moral as
   well as political delicacy, and it is not meant here to examine it. It
25 is only important at the present occasion, to observe that to
   generalize such a principle and to think of reducing it to a System
   ... is a Scheme utterly impracticable and objectionable ... No

Country having a Representative system of Govt. could act upon
it, and the sooner such a Doctrine shall be distinctly abjured as
30 forming in any Degree the Basis of our Alliance, the better. . . .

Castlereagh was also averse to the attempt to endow the Alliance with
some form of moral force. Where he differed from most of his insular
colleagues, was in his genuine belief in the merits of periodic meetings,
based on his experience of successful cooperation from 1813 to 1815.
Canning lacked this experience of the value of personal contact and also
disliked Metternich. He therefore regarded the split in the Alliance at
Verona as a return to 'a wholesome state again', rejoicing that it was,
once more, a case of 'Every nation for itself and God for us all'. Such
sentiments, which were warmly approved by Parliament, clearly
signified the end of Britain's participation in the Congress System.

5 The Congress System – A Failure?

There is general agreement among historians that there was no real
'system' to the series of congresses held between 1818 and 1822. It is
suggested that, by itself, the idea of periodic meetings was an insuf-
ficient basis for a successful experiment in international cooperation.
Without a permanent organisation to collect material for preliminary
consideration, to prepare an agenda and to establish agreed rules of
procedure at the meetings, the congresses were incapable of operating
in anything but an *ad hoc*, amateurish fashion. Metternich himself
seems to have realised this by 1823 when he commented to an adviser:
'before talking about congresses it is necessary to come to an accord on
many matters, and the way to do this is through simple conferences'.
The Congress System was perhaps too ambitious in attempting to
secure the agreement of all five Great Powers on the range of issues that
came before them.

The Congress System has also been seen as a 'missed opportunity' for
making adjustments to the Vienna Settlement in the light of subsequent
events. Once it became clear that there were popular pressures for good
government and for some recognition of national identity, the Congress
System, it has been suggested, provided a suitable forum for consideration of modifications to the peace treaty. Instead, the majority of the
Great Powers were persuaded by Metternich to adopt an essentially
static concept of how to preserve peace and stability, which sought to
repress popular movements rather than make concessions to liberal or
nationalist aspirations. The three eastern powers, in particular, seemed
to be unable to differentiate between demands for constitutional reform
and the sort of militant jacobinism that had caused much of the unrest
in Europe in the 1790s. British public opinion would not permit its
government to support the sort of gross misgovernment that characterised the rule of Ferdinand of Spain, but the continuance of the

Congress System without Britain, one of the two leading Great Powers, would have been nonsensical.

A fatal flaw in the Congress System was the failure to establish agreed principles on which the Alliance of the Great Powers was supposed to operate. Consequently, problems arose from the existence of too many principles which were not readily compatible. Thus Article VI of the treaty of November 1815 sought to establish the idea of periodic meetings to discuss matters of common concern. The Tsar's Holy Alliance attempted to give Castlereagh's essentially practical scheme a sort of moralistic nature, while Metternich's Troppau Protocol gave the Tsar's fairly innocuous pious sentiments a thoroughly repressive twist. Castlereagh understandably objected to what he regarded as the perversion of the principle of the Alliance, whose terms, he believed, had been laid down in 1815. This appears to have been the crux of the matter – that what was constituted in 1815 was an Alliance, directed (in Britain's view, at least) against a possible revival of French militarism, with an added proviso for future meetings. However, the Tsar had confused the issue prior to this treaty of November 1815, with his Holy Alliance scheme in September. This may help to explain why the divergence of views which emerged in 1820 seemed to puzzle and annoy the leading participants in the Congress System, since they believed that its basic principles had been agreed upon in 1815.

The most obvious failure of the Congress System was its lack of flexibility. As a forum for cooperation among the Great Powers, its inability to accommodate differing views of what constituted a serious danger to the peace of Europe was fatal to its survival. The revolts in Spain, Naples, and Greece split the five-power Alliance in different ways – the three powers who tried to resolve the Greek revolt being a quite different combination from the three who agreed to the suppression of the Neapolitan revolt in the name of the Alliance. The Congress System could not operate effectively in such a situation.

Although the Congress System did not cope very well with some of the problems in international affairs from 1815 to 1822, some useful things were achieved during this period. The basis for a stable international order was created. France was re-integrated into the diplomatic community only three years after the end of the war, without destroying the Quadruple Alliance as a precaution against a resurgence of French aggression. Cooperation between Austria and Britain from 1815 to 1820 helped to maintain stability in Europe by keeping both France and Russia in check. When Anglo-Austrian cooperation broke down, in 1820, it was possible by then for Austria to look to Russia for aid in defending the conservative, monarchical order on the continent. By this time, Russia was no longer regarded as an expansionist power but as being committed to the defence of the status quo against the spread of liberal and revolutionary ideas. The protection she afforded to the two other conservative powers, Austria and

Prussia, therefore helped to consolidate the territorial system created in 1815.

In recent years some historians have suggested that too much prominence has been given to the working of the Congress System in the study of international affairs in the period 1815–23, to the neglect of important underlying issues in Great Power relations, such as the Franco–Russian alignment. The congresses themselves might be better regarded, perhaps, as the tip of the iceberg of the diplomatic activity of these years, much of which was conducted beneath the level of 'high powered' meetings attended by the monarchs and foreign ministers of the Great Powers.

The years 1815 to 1823 represent a phase in Great Power relations when diplomatic gatherings to discuss matters of common concern mainly took the form of congresses. The inspiration for this experiment was mainly the experience of successful diplomatic cooperation from 1813 to 1815. The novelty was the attempt to continue this experience in peacetime. As an experiment, the Congress System was not so much a forerunner of the League of Nations (although there was undoubtedly an attempt by the Tsar to make it into a sort of European Government) as an early form of 'Summit Diplomacy'. The success of this type of diplomacy appears to depend on personal relationships, careful preparation and agreement on basic objectives. The Congress System seems to have possessed only one of those three attributes, and even that disappeared with Castlereagh's death in 1822, followed by the death of Alexander in 1825.

6 Alternatives to Congress Diplomacy

Between the breakdown of the Congress System in 1823 and the revolutions of 1830, international relations were in a state of flux. The Great Powers were clearly at odds over the question of what should be done about revolutions. After the Troppau Protocol had pronounced a blanket condemnation of all revolutions, cooperation between Britain and the other powers was almost impossible on most issues. This was not because the Tory government in Britain favoured revolutionary upheavals – far from it. But liberal opinion in Britain was sympathetic to movements seeking constitutional change in a reasonably ordered fashion in the smaller states. Canning was happy to see the Congress System collapse, partly because he was more openly 'liberal' in sentiment than Castlereagh and partly because he preferred to defend British interests by direct, face to face negotiations with individual statesmen. Although the limitations of this approach were to become apparent with the Greek revolt, Canning's use of direct negotiations was very successful in protecting British interests in Portugal, her Brazilian colony and in the Spanish colonies of Latin America.

The rebellion against Spanish rule in Latin America which began in

1810 had profited from Spain's involvement in the Napoleonic Wars and her preoccupation with the revolt in 1820 against the absolutist King Ferdinand. Britain's trade with Latin America had expanded greatly during the wars, when European markets had been disrupted, or even closed to British commerce. It had also benefited from the loosening of Spain's political and economic control over her colonies in wartime. The French invasion of Spain in April 1823 to restore royal authority was seen as a threat to British interests in two ways. Firstly, French armies might go on to invade Portugal to assist the absolutist cause there. Secondly, it was feared that France would assist Ferdinand to reassert complete control over his rebellious colonies.

Canning averted the danger to British interests in April 1823 by securing assurances from France on three points: the occupation of Spain would be temporary; Portugal's integrity would be respected; and force would not be used against the rebellious Spanish colonies. However, the advance of the French army in September 1823 to Cadiz, the main port for colonial traffic, led Canning to threaten France with war if she broke her word and attempted to extend the scope of her intervention to include the colonies. Direct negotiations once more proved effective. In the Polignac Agreement of October 1823, the French government disclaimed any intention to recover Spain's colonies or to seek exclusive advantages there for herself.

Prior to this, Canning had approached the United States for a joint declaration against European interference in Latin America, but with no success. The Americans believed they had more to fear from British trade and influence than from France or Russia – whose claim to territory from Alaska to 'British Columbia' was not taken seriously. The declaration by the American President in December 1823 that European interference in the affairs of the Americas would be regarded as an 'unfriendly act' (the Monroe Doctrine, as it came to be called) was somewhat fraudulent, since it depended on British sea power to be effective. A year later, the British government finally decided to recognise the Spanish colonies as independent republics, followed soon after by recognition of Brazil's independence from Portugal. Canning's boast, 'I have called the New World into existence to redress the balance of the Old', is more memorable than informative. The meaning is more obvious from the context, in that it concluded a speech made later, in 1826, in which Canning asserted: 'I looked to America to redress the inequalities of Europe. Contemplating Spain, such as our ancestors had known her, I resolved that, if France had Spain, it should not be Spain with "the Indies".'

The Old World, in the shape of Spain and the Holy Alliance powers, strongly protested against the recognition of rebel regimes and held a conference in Paris in 1826 to discuss the affairs of Spain and her colonies. Canning declined the invitation to this conference because it proposed to discuss the threat to 'the security of Spain' of recent events in Portugal, which Canning regarded as a British preserve. On the death of King John of Portugal in 1826, his successor granted a Charter of Liberties to his subjects before abdicating in favour of his infant daughter, assisted by a Regency Council. The three eastern powers expressed alarm at this encouragement of constitutionalism, fearing its effect on Spanish politics, but they could hardly condemn the legitimate action of the Portuguese monarch. Instead, they encouraged Spain to provide unofficial military aid to the absolutist forces in Portugal to enable Miguel (King John's second son) to overthrow the Regency and establish an absolutist regime. In December 1826 Canning responded to Portuguese appeals for aid by despatching a force of 4,000 British troops to support the legal government. Faced with this display of British determination, the Spanish government ceased its covert aid to the Miguelites, temporarily at least.

Between 1823 and 1826, therefore, Canning had successfully defended British interests by unilateral action, diplomatic and military, spurning Metternich's proposals for conferences. However, modern historians are somewhat sceptical of the traditional view that Canning was a zealous supporter of either colonial independence or continental liberalism. As he himself once remarked: 'Let us not, in the foolish spirit of romance, suppose that we alone could regenerate Europe'. His main concern, it is now believed, as regards Latin America was British trade. In the case of Portugal, with whom Britain had centuries-old ties of friendship, it was Britain's prestige that he was upholding by preventing Spain (backed by France) from determining the political fate of Britain's oldest ally. What Canning achieved was, in effect, a tacit understanding with France that her influence in Spain would be matched by British influence in Portuguese affairs. The decisive factor in the success of his policies towards both Portugal and the Spanish colonies was, of course, British sea power. The weakness of his approach was that if the other powers followed his example and pursued their own interests exclusively, the whole concept of Great Power cooperation within the Concert of Europe would be destroyed.

  * Canning's exclusive reliance on direct negotiations denied the possibility of an alternative basis for international cooperation in the form of ambassadorial conferences. After 1823, conferences took the place of congresses as the forum for deliberations among the Great Powers. Because they dealt with one specific issue and did not require the presence of all five states, they tended to be more effective than the congresses had been.

The merits of 'Conference Diplomacy', as it is sometimes called, were evident in the later stages of the Greek revolt. On a major issue such as the Eastern Question, the limitations of Canning's 'everyone for himself' approach were severe. The Near East was an area where international understanding was most needed since several of the powers had important interests to defend there. But in 1825, Count Nesselrode became impatient at the obstructive attitude of the other

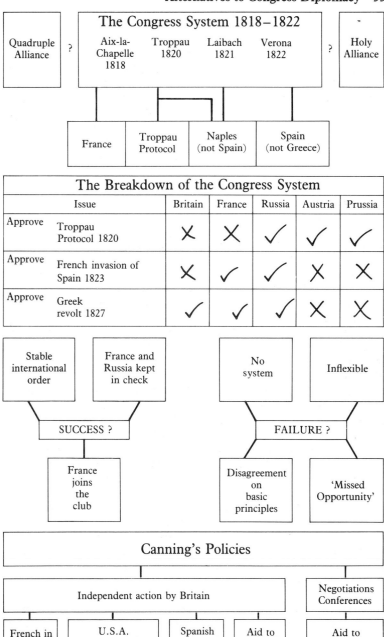

The Congress System 1818–1822

| Quadruple Alliance | ? | Aix-la-Chapelle 1818 | Troppau 1820 | Laibach 1821 | Verona 1822 | ? | Holy Alliance |

| France | Troppau Protocol | Naples (not Spain) | Spain (not Greece) |

The Breakdown of the Congress System

	Issue	Britain	France	Russia	Austria	Prussia
Approve	Troppau Protocol 1820	✗	✗	✓	✓	✓
Approve	French invasion of Spain 1823	✗	✓	✓	✗	✗
Approve	Greek revolt 1827	✓	✓	✓	✗	✗

| Stable international order | France and Russia kept in check | | No system | Inflexible |

| SUCCESS ? | | FAILURE ? |

| France joins the club | | Disagreement on basic principles | 'Missed Opportunity' |

Canning's Policies

| Independent action by Britain | | | | Negotiations Conferences |

| French in Spain 1823 | U.S.A. Monroe Doctrine 1823 | Spanish Colonies 1824 | Aid to Portugal 1826 | Aid to Greeks 1827–1830 |

Summary – The Congress System

powers towards Russian proposals for mediation in the Greek revolt, and asserted in a Circular to Russian embassies abroad that: 'Russia will follow her own views exclusively and will be governed by her own interests'.

The Nesselrode Circular of August 1825 was tantamount to a repudiation of the whole concept of the Concert of Europe and would also have led to war, if acted upon. Fortunately, by 1826 Canning recognised the need to cooperate with Russia, if only to forestall unilateral Russian action against the Turks. An Anglo-Russian accord, on the basis of an autonomous Greek state, was concluded in St Petersburg in April 1826, to which France acceded in the following year. The Treaty of London of July 1827 and the subsequent ambassadorial conference therefore represents a return to the paths of international cooperation, in that it brought together Russia, Britain and France in an agreed solution to the Greek revolt. Although Austria and Prussia refused to be a party to this agreement, something had been salvaged from the wreck of the Congress System – a willingness to persevere with diplomatic cooperation to avoid the danger of war among the Great Powers.

Making notes on 'The Congress System'

Once again, your notes on this chapter need to provide you with a sufficient record for revision purposes. You will need both a record of the facts (what happened) and an outline of the issues that have interested historians (the patterns that have been made of the facts). You may find it helpful to use the same sequence of headings as in the chapter.

1. Introduction. Was there a Congress 'System'?
2. Origins of the Congress System.
3. The Congresses. In the sub-section on the Congress of Troppau you should make separate notes on the revolts of 1820, and the Troppau Protocol.
4. The Breakdown of the Congress System. Distinguish between the 'occasion' (Spain and Greece) and the 'causes'.
5. The Congress System – A Failure? In what ways was it a) a success and b) a failure? What were the reasons for its successes and failures?
6. Alternatives to Congress Diplomacy. What was 'Conference Diplomacy'? Explain how and why it was used by Canning and his successors up to 1830.

Answering essay questions on 'The Congress System'

The Congress System is another very popular topic among examiners. You are most likely to be asked to discuss either a) what it was (aims and methods), b) its success or failure, or c) the reasons for its decline. Look carefully at the following 'challenging statement' questions.

1. '"Both in intention and effect, the Congress System merely sustained the restored *ancien régime* in Europe." How far do you agree with this verdict?'
2. '"The Congress System was a praiseworthy effort to maintain peace by international cooperation." How much justification is there in this verdict?'
3. '"The conflicting interests of the Great Powers made its failure inevitable." Discuss this verdict on the Congress System.'
4. '"The Congress System foundered on the reef of the Eastern Question." Do you agree?'
5. '"The Congress System achieved nothing of lasting value." How fair is this assessment of its achievements?'
6. 'Discuss the opinion that "the Congress System scarcely justifies the attention it has received from historians".'

Which of the questions are about the reasons for the decline of the Congress System? What reason is suggested in question 3? List the other reasons that should be discussed in answering this question.

You should now be in a good position to draw up a detailed plan for an answer to question 3. The plan for the main body of the essay is almost self-evident. There should be one paragraph on each of the reasons you have identified, starting with the one suggested in the question. What system of 'ordering' the paragraphs would you use?

The introductory paragraph in 'challenging statement' essays is more important than is often the case with other types of essay. Besides the normal statement about what you are intending to do in the essay – for example, 'The Congress System failed for many reasons, including the conflicting interests of the Great Powers. In this essay the major reasons will be identified and their relative importance will be assessed' – there is also the need both to draw attention to and comment on any of the assumptions made in the question that are at all controversial, and to define any terms that are ambiguous or unclear. In question 3 'failure' and 'inevitable' might need comment. What in question 2 would need similar treatment?

Further stages of dealing with 'challenging statement' questions will be discussed on page 110.

Source-based questions on 'The Congress System'

1 The origins of the Congress System
Carefully read the extracts from the Treaty of Chaumont, the Quadruple Alliance, and the Holy Alliance given on pages 39–40. Answer the following questions:
a) What is meant by 'to themselves reciprocally' in the first extract on page 39, 'the most salutary for the repose and prosperity of Nations' in the second extract on page 39, and 'true and indissoluble fraternity' in the third extract on page 40? (6 marks)
b) Rank the three extracts in terms of their preciseness or vagueness, ranking the most explicit highest and the most general lowest. (3 marks)
c) What can be learnt from the extracts about the aims of the Treaty of Chaumont, the Quadruple Alliance and the Holy Alliance? (6 marks)
d) What is it about the extracts that marks them out as being from international agreements rather than from letters, memoirs or memoranda? Illustrate your answer with short quotations from all three extracts. (6 marks)
e) Agreements such as the three featured in the extracts are often somewhat vague. What is the most likely explanation for this common feature? (4 marks)

2 Intervention in the affairs of other states
Carefully read the extracts from the Troppau Protocol, the Circular of November 1820, and Castlereagh's State Paper given on pages 44–5 and 49–50. Answer the following questions:
a) In what chronological order did the three documents originate? (3 marks)
b) What appears to have been the purpose of i) the Circular of November 1820, and ii) Castlereagh's State Paper? Support your answers with brief extracts from the documents. (8 marks)
c) How accurate a predictor of Britain's reaction to the Troppau Protocol is Castlereagh's State Paper? Explain your answer. (4 marks)
d) The Troppau Protocol contains several qualifying conditions that would need to apply in any case before the agreement would come into effect. Quote three examples of these, and from your knowledge of the political situation at the time speculate on the likely reasons for their inclusion. (6 marks)
e) What evidence might historians seek in order to assess the accuracy of the speculations you have made in answer to the last question? (4 marks)

CHAPTER 4

The Revolutions of 1830 and 1848

1 Introduction

In 1830 revolutions broke out in France, Belgium and Poland, followed by risings in central Italy and localised revolts in some German states. Crises arose also in the Near East in the early and late 1830s which had an important influence on relations between the Great Powers (see pages 86–91). In addition, the 1830s saw a revival of the struggle between constitutionalists and absolutists in both Spain and Portugal, in which France and Britain became once again involved.

Between 1830 and 1848 two major issues in international affairs, the Belgian revolt and the Eastern Question, were settled by means of 'Conference Diplomacy'. Conferences were held in one of the European capitals, usually London or Vienna, with the resident ambassadors acting as the representatives of their countries, under the chairmanship of the host foreign minister. This form of diplomatic cooperation was not based on a prejudgement of the merits of a situation. Unlike the Congress System's condemnation of revolution, it was 'ideologically neutral'. It was little more than an agreed strategy for resolving important problems by round-table discussions with a willingness to accept an outcome that was less than ideal, if necessary, for the sake of reaching an agreement and preserving peace. However, this is not to suggest that international relations were characterised by sweetness and light from 1830 to 1848. Far from it. Serious disagreements existed, crises verging on war arose and personal animosities abounded. Some of this is attributable to the abrasive manner sometimes adopted by Palmerston, the new British Foreign Secretary from November 1830, who was a worthy rival to Metternich. Despite this, the Concert of Europe took on a new lease of life after 1830, even though the 1830 revolution in France inaugurated a liberal regime emphasising the ideological divide between the western and eastern powers.

2 The Revolutions of 1830–1

a) The Revolution of 1830 in France

The 1830 revolution in France ended the rule of the Bourbon monarch Charles X, whose reactionary domestic policies culminated in the violation of the Charter of 1814. The July revolution brought to power Louis-Philippe, representative of the Orléanist (younger) branch of the French royal family. His accession disappointed the hopes of the Republicans who, although active in Paris, lacked mass support in the provinces. The change of regime in France had a significant impact on international relations for at least a decade.

The outbreak of revolution in France naturally alarmed the three eastern powers who renewed their pledges to sustain the 1815 treaties. Although they made warlike preparations, they reluctantly accepted the situation and merely warned France against any attempt to disturb the European status quo. In Austria's case, the Emperor's decision to recognise the new regime in France stemmed from the realisation that his army was in no fit state for war. The Tsar, however, refused to recognise Louis-Philippe as King until January 1831, souring relations to such an extent that a Franco-Russian alignment ceased to be regarded as a serious possibility for nearly 20 years. The revolution in France also served to strengthen the coherence of the union of the eastern powers, which had been weakened by disagreements over the Greek revolt in the late 1820s.

  * In Britain, by contrast, the change of regime in France was welcomed – especially by the new Whig government which replaced Wellington's Tory administration in November 1830. The new Foreign Secretary, Palmerston, was eager to promote an Anglo-French entente, committed to the defence of liberalism in Europe against the absolutist powers of the 'Holy Alliance'. At the same time, his willingness to maintain friendly relations with France was conditional on her respect for the 1815 settlement and on French support for British policy in the Near East. Although this 'Liberal Alliance' had some impact on international affairs in the early 1830s, French governments found the role of junior partner to Britain increasingly irksome. By the end of the decade, therefore, the ideological division between east and west, which was never completely rigid, was giving way to a more flexible set of relationships.

The lack of total rigidity in great power alignments was evident as early as 1830–1, in the peaceful solution of the Belgian Question. A key factor here was not only the newly created entente between Britain and France, but also the support Palmerston was able to call upon from the Holy Alliance powers to impose restraint on French ambitions to secure advantages for herself.

b) The Belgian Revolt of 1830

The union of the former Austrian Netherlands with the Kingdom of Holland had been decreed in 1815 on military and strategic grounds. Even so, it was not an unworkable arrangement despite the fact that the southern Catholic provinces of Belgium had led a separate political existence from Calvinist Holland since the north–south division of the Netherlands in the early seventeenth century. The discontent with Dutch rule that arose in the late 1820s, encouraged by French agents, was mainly due to grievances over religion, taxation and the predominance of the Dutch language and Dutch officials. A riot in Brussels in late August 1830, following the July Revolution in Paris, escalated into a revolt when Dutch troops were sent to restore order. By September, most of Belgium was in revolt and a provisional government had been set up.

The revolt directly challenged one of the arrangements made in the Treaty of Vienna to create a barrier against French expansion, so the appeal of the King of Holland for aid against his rebellious subjects was unlikely to be ignored by the Great Powers. Britain's main concern was to ensure that the Belgian ports did not fall into the hands of a Great Power, such as France. The King's appeal was also bound to produce a sympathetic response from the three eastern powers. As well as upholding the Vienna Treaty, they were staunch supporters of monarchical rights and enemies of revolution. The Belgians, on the other hand, expected the new liberal regime in France to prevent the suppression of the revolt by force. If Prussian troops went to the aid of King William of Holland, popular pressure in France would almost certainly force Louis-Philippe to send a French army to assist the Belgians and the Great Powers would then find themselves drawn into a European war. It was, as the Duke of Wellington, then Prime Minister of Britain, remarked: 'a devilish bad business, the most serious affair for Europe that could have arisen'.

The immediate danger of a conflict among the Great Powers was avoided when the Prussians accepted a French proposal for non-intervention, made in October 1830, after the Belgians had proclaimed their independence from Holland. In early November, the Dutch King and the other powers agreed to an Anglo-French proposal for a conference of ambassadors in London. The initial successes of the London Conference owed much to the cooperation of Talleyrand, the new French ambassador to London, with Palmerston, the new British Foreign Secretary. Even so, the compliance of the eastern powers was not fully assured until late November 1830, when a revolt broke out in Poland. Thereafter, Russia was preoccupied with quelling that revolt, and saw little prospect of successful intervention on Holland's side while Britain and France were in accord. Since the Austrians were unwilling to act without Russia, and Prussia wished to avoid confrontation with Britain, agreement was secured on the basic issue of seeking a negotiated settlement.

In November 1830 the London Conference agreed on an armistice to localise the conflict, followed shortly afterwards by acceptance of the fact of Belgian independence and, in early 1831, its neutrality. Thereafter, the Great Powers encountered endless difficulties over the terms of the separation of Belgium from Holland. Added to the technical problems of a financial and economic nature, were a lengthy dispute over boundaries and the politically sensitive issue of a new monarch for Belgium. Eventually, Leopold of Saxe-Coburg, an uncle of the future

Queen Victoria, was accepted as a 'neutral' candidate for the Belgian throne.

After this, two major problems complicated the work of the Conference, delaying its completion until the spring of 1832. Firstly, France found it hard to resist the temptation of seeking territorial gains or other advantages for herself, despite a self-denying agreement made by the five Great Powers. She laid claim to Luxembourg and was tempted to accept the offer of the Belgian crown to a younger son of Louis-Philippe. Secondly, not only did the Dutch King adopt an obstructive attitude on most issues and have to be coerced into accepting the terms arrived at by the Conference, but the Belgians were almost equally intransigent at times. The Great Powers issued a collective ultimatum to the Dutch King, warning him that 'the rejection of their demands would be considered by the Five Powers as an act of hostility against them', while the Belgians were reproved for their failure to be realistic about the terms of their separation from Holland.

After the Belgians, under pressure, accepted the terms of the settlement in June 1831, it was the turn of the Dutch to be recalcitrant. When their troops marched on Brussels in August, the Great Powers gave approval to the despatch of a French army and a British naval squadron to force the Dutch to retreat. But the presence of French troops in Belgium encouraged French aspirations for territorial gains and the possibility of partitioning Belgium, until a British threat of war, backed by the other powers, persuaded them reluctantly to withdraw. Palmerston's warning was quite blunt: 'the French must go out of Belgium or we shall have a general war, and war in a few days'. By November 1831, the Great Powers were able to conclude a treaty with Belgium which recognised her existence as part of the European state system. Dutch obstinacy persisted, however, so that another Anglo-French operation, with the consent of the other powers, was needed in December 1832 to evict the Dutch from Antwerp. In May 1833, the King of Holland eventually consented to a truce, but it was not until 1839 that he finally accepted the independence of Belgium. The Great Powers were then able to guarantee Belgium's permanent neutrality. Much of the credit for this successful outcome belongs to Palmerston for his mastery of detail, combined with firmness and flexibility towards what an exasperated colleague called 'these damned Dutch and Belgians'.

The London Conference was also a remarkable display of collective responsibility on the part of the Great Powers, some of whom had considerable misgivings about the coercion of a legitimate ruler in order to set up an independent Belgium, contrary to the provisions of the Vienna Treaty. It was undoubtedly a triumph for the Concert of Europe that the need for change was accepted and war avoided. This showed the advantages which the flexibility of 'Conference Diplomacy' had brought to international relations.

c) The Polish and Italian Revolts of 1830–1

The Polish revolt of 1830–1 began when the Tsar ordered a general mobilisation to deal with the potential revolutionary threat from France. In late November 1830 the Warsaw garrison, led by its junior officers, rose in revolt against Russian rule. The rising was inspired by a sort of romantic nationalism disseminated through secret societies to which young officers and cadets belonged, as well as through student fraternities in Warsaw and Vilna.

The strength of the revolt lay in the backing of the Polish army which initially outnumbered the Russian forces in Poland, enabling the rebellion to win some early successes. Its weaknesses resulted from the lack of mass support, especially from the peasantry, and the split between moderate and radical revolutionary groups. Whereas the moderates hoped to win concessions from the Tsar, the radicals demanded complete national independence. Patriotic Poles naturally resented Russian rule, but the relatively mild nature of that rule since 1815 meant that the masses had not been antagonised by it. They suffered more from the burdens imposed on them by the Polish landowners, who were the leaders of the revolt, so they had little reason to support those who were their main oppressors. In the late spring of 1831, the tide turned in Russia's favour and in September Warsaw fell to the advancing Russian armies. The revolt was followed by harsh retribution. Poland was placed under military rule which abolished the Diet, the universities and the separate Polish army. A policy of Russification, including the use of the Russian language in schools, was vigorously applied to weaken Polish nationalism.

The Poles had assumed that the western powers would come to their aid. They asserted that Poland had superior claims to national independence on historical grounds than either the Greeks or the Belgians, whose claims to nationhood had recently been championed by Britain and France. The Poles' argument was indeed well founded, but it ignored the harsh realities of political life. Belgium was part of western Europe, whose political fate could not be determined by the Holy Alliance powers if Britain and France stood together. Furthermore, the western powers could use their sea power to good effect to coerce the Sultan of Turkey and the King of Holland but, as Palmerston bluntly observed to a Polish leader: 'We cannot send an army to Poland and the burning of the Russian fleet would be about as effectual as the burning of Moscow'.

France, the benefactor of Poland in the Napoleonic era, felt a stronger obligation towards the Poles, but the new regime could not afford the risks involved in a crusade to liberate Poland. The Russian army was too formidable an opponent even for France, who contented herself with diplomatic gestures, condemning Russian action in Poland and proposing a conference of the Great Powers to urge Russia to make concessions to Polish demands. Despite British sympathy for the Poles, Palmerston did not wish to challenge Russia's right to rule over Poland which was founded on the treaties of 1815, one of whose objects was to keep France in check! Poland's misfortune was to belong, politically and geographically, to eastern Europe, which was regarded as a Russian sphere of influence and it was not in Britain's interest to undermine the existing international order.

* Whether Italy could similarly be regarded as Austria's sphere of influence, to the exclusion of other powers, was put to the test by the risings of 1831 in the duchies of Parma and Modena and in the Papal States. The conspirators, encouraged by signs that France intended to oppose Austrian interference in the affairs of the Italian states, began their campaign for a Union of Central Italy in February 1831. Provisional governments were set up, but the movement for union was ill-coordinated and weakened by local loyalties and rivalries. Austrian troops quickly suppressed the risings in March 1831, but they had to return to the Papal States a year later to deal with another uprising. This provoked the despatch of a French force to the papal port of Ancona in February 1832, remaining in occupation there until 1838 when the Austrian troops finally evacuated Bologna. France's symbolic gesture of defiance against Austria was meant to assert her right to pose as the patron of reform movements in Italy. It was not meant to challenge Austria to the point of war, as Palmerston feared.

3 Spain and Portugal in the 1830s and 1840s

The struggles of the 1820s between constitutionalists and absolutists in Spain and Portugal persisted during the two following decades. The withdrawal of British troops from Portugal in 1827 had resulted in the triumph of the absolutists, backed by Spain, over the constitutionalists. This had enabled Miguel to become King. Then in the 1830s it was Spain's turn to suffer a succession dispute when, on the death of Ferdinand in September 1833, his brother Don Carlos claimed the throne.

Since Carlos was supported by absolutists in both Spain and Portugal, the widowed Queen, acting as Regent for her young daughter, Isabella, turned to the constitutionalists for support. The liberal regime of Louis-Philippe, which had come to power in France in July 1830, was willing to cooperate with Britain to assist the constitutionalist cause but Palmerston added to the confusion by refusing to cooperate with the French on a straightforward basis of equal rights. In fairness, France should have been allowed to assist the constitutionalists in Spain, just as Britain claimed the right to support their cause in Portugal, but Palmerston intended otherwise. Although he wanted to create a 'Western Confederacy' to defend liberal institutions, he distrusted the French. This is why early in 1834, he had rejected a

French offer of a general alliance because he suspected that, once assured of British support, France would attempt to realise her territorial ambitions. However, in the spring of 1834, he agreed to a Quadruple Alliance between Britain, France, Portugal and Spain in defence of liberal institutions, but with France in a subordinate position to Britain. This was made clear in the treaty, in that whereas Britain was to act alone in Portugal, France was not entitled to intervene in Spain unless specifically invited to do so.

In accordance with the treaty, the destruction of the absolutist forces of both King Miguel and the Spanish pretender, Don Carlos, located inside Portugal, was accomplished by the Spanish army and British naval forces in the spring of 1834. It seemed therefore as if the Quadruple Alliance had been a great success in championing the liberal cause, realising Palmerston's hopes that it would be a 'powerful counterpoise' to the Holy Alliance.

The reality was quite different. In fact, the liberal cause was not firmly established in Spain, and the unity of the Quadruple Alliance was undermined by endless recriminations among its members. The Spanish liberals encountered fresh difficulties when Don Carlos returned secretly to Spain to renew his claim to the throne and raised a new army in the north of the country. The 'Carlists', as they were called, joined forces with the Basques who were engaged in guerrilla warfare in support of their demands for regional liberties. Neither of the two Great Powers was keen to become involved in this type of provincial civil war, in which conventional military operations were unlikely to be effective. They therefore refused the Spanish Queen's appeals for official military aid in 1835, sending token forces of volunteers or irregular troops instead. The recriminations between Britain and France stemmed from Palmerston's reluctance to allow France the opportunity to restore her influence at Madrid by lending more effective aid to the liberal cause. As a result, Anglo-French cooperation had turned into rivalry by 1836, which persisted for the next decade.

* The politics of the Iberian Peninsula remained unsettled in the late 1830s and early 1840s. This was partly because of the rivalry between Britain and France and partly because their refusal to furnish the sort of military aid demanded by the constitutionalists in Spain prolonged the political unrest. In Madrid, British influence was dominant until 1844, when the pro-French party ousted their rivals. France then attempted to consolidate her position by arranging marriages for the young Queen and her sister in such a way as to perpetuate French influence in Spain. Once the Queen was married to a Spanish nobleman, who was reputed to be impotent, her sister was to marry a younger son of Louis-Philippe. This arrangement was acceptable to the Conservative Foreign Secretary, Lord Aberdeen, but on Palmerston's return to office in 1846 this amicable agreement ended abruptly. The French retaliated by

pressing the Spanish government to agree to the simultaneous marriages of the Queen and her sister, heiress to the throne. Palmerston's anger at what he regarded as French duplicity made Anglo-French cooperation in Iberian affairs more difficult than ever.

This unseemly wrangle had an effect on attitudes towards the latest disorders in Portugal in 1846–7 where the Queen and her ministers made themselves unpopular by resorting to arbitrary measures. Palmerston's proposal for reforms to win back the allegiance of the radicals (advanced liberals) to the government was rejected on the grounds that the revolt had been taken over by the Miguelites! Although exaggerated, there was probably some truth in the assertion.

British sympathy for the radical protesters, civilian and military, was interpreted by the French and Spanish governments as an attempt to encourage radical (anti-French) dissidents in Spain. Both France and Spain therefore supported the Portuguese request for assistance, under the treaty of April 1834, to suppress the (allegedly Miguelite) rebellion. The refusal of the rebels to compromise left Palmerston no option but to agree to joint intervention in Portugal. Accordingly, in July 1847, Spanish troops and an Anglo-French naval force destroyed the rebel army and its bases. British influence at Lisbon was thereby preserved, but only through the type of action which, as Palmerston conceded, was 'a very unusual measure for the British government to take'.

4 The Concert and Diplomatic Alignments 1830–48

The apparent division of the Great Powers after 1830 into two opposing ideological camps – the Liberal Alliance and the Holy Alliance – contained a potential threat to the working of the Concert of Europe. The success of the Concert depended, after all, on a degree of consensus amongst the five Great Powers and a willingness to resolve problems of common concern by negotiation. Fortunately, in the 1830s and 1840s a remarkable degree of flexibility developed in the alignment of the powers on some issues, despite their ideological differences, which contributed to the continuing vitality of the Concert of Europe.

The re-emergence of revolutionary tendencies in the early 1830s served to consolidate the grouping of the three eastern powers, which had been weakened by disagreements over the Eastern Question in the late 1820s (see page 84). In the Münchengrätz Agreement of September 1833, the Tsar gave Metternich assurances that Russia harboured no expansionist designs on either Turkey or Poland. A mutual guarantee of their Polish possessions was accompanied by an agreement to work together to maintain the integrity of the Ottoman Empire. A further treaty, the Convention of Berlin (October 1833) in which Prussia participated, was based on principles reminiscent of the Troppau Protocol of 1820. The three monarchs, who constituted the so-called 'three Northern Courts', promised to assist each other in the suppression of revolution. They also agreed to prevent 'counter-intervention' by a fourth power, such as France, whose occupation of Ancona in 1832 had annoyed Austria. By these agreements, the three eastern powers asserted their solidarity and their determination to defend the status quo.

An opportunity for the western powers to demonstrate the strength of their partnership came with the renewal of political struggles in the Iberian Peninsula in the early 1830s. The Quadruple Alliance of 1834, however, was greatly weakened by mutual recriminations within two years. Anglo-French relations deteriorated even further with the renewal of the Mehemet Ali affair in 1839–41 (see page 89). Indeed, at the height of the crisis in 1840 some observers believed that war between the two powers was almost certain. In contrast, cooperation between Britain and Russia over this issue led to a dramatic improvement in Anglo–Russian relations, symbolised by the Tsar's visit to England in 1844. In view of Palmerston's deep suspicion of, and hostility towards, Russia in the 1830s, his willingness to cooperate with her in the Near East in 1839–41 was a major *volte face*, underlining the flexibility of alignments in this period.

However, the Anglo-French entente did recover some of its former cordiality between 1841 and 1846, when Aberdeen and Guizot attempted to work more closely over issues such as Spain. This cordiality came to a sudden end on Palmerston's return to office and his abrupt reaction to the 'Spanish Marriages' affair, influencing attitudes towards the issue of intervention in Portugal. Although the western powers liked to pretend that they were only intervening in Spain and Portugal to preserve the 'independence' of these states, in reality they were supporting a particular type of regime – 'after the fashions of Austria and Russia', as Palmerston ruefully admitted in 1847. In this respect the earlier distinction between the two groupings of the Great Powers had also become somewhat blurred by the 1840s.

In the late 1840s the 'ideological divide', represented by the Liberal Alliance and the Holy Alliance, almost ceased to have any significance in the relations between the Great Powers. The very fact that from 1846 to 1848 Britain and France were at loggerheads enabled Austria and Russia to suppress a rising in the Republic of Cracow in Poland, thereby ending its independence agreed in the 1815 treaties, without fear of a serious riposte from the west. The breakdown of the Anglo-French entente also led both partners to seek better relations with Russia and Austria respectively. For example, Guizot informed Vienna in May 1847 that 'France is now disposed and suited to a policy of conservatism' as a sign of his desire for a *rapprochement* with Austria.

Political unrest in Switzerland and in central Italy in 1847 seemed to present opportunities for Franco-Austrian cooperation in the interests of stability in Europe. In the event, the French failed to convince

Metternich that their conversion to 'a policy of conservatism' was really genuine. Nevertheless, despite its failure, the fact that such cooperation was attempted on the eve of 1848 is remarkable in itself, given that in 1830 the Austrians had wanted to invade France to dethrone the 'usurper', Louis-Philippe. However, it was the willingness of Britain and Russia to work together in the interests of peace, after the outbreak of revolutions in 1848, which was the really significant outcome of the changing alignments of the Great Powers between 1815 and 1848.

5 The Revolutions of 1848–9

In the spring of 1848, a wave of revolutions swept across much of Europe. Following the overthrow of the Orléanist monarchy in France in late February, revolutions broke out in Italy, the German states and Austria and Prussia. Of the Great Powers, only liberal Britain and autocratic Russia were immune to the revolutionary fever. 1848 was the springtide of liberalism and nationalism in Europe, symbolised by the dismissal of Metternich and the acceptance of the German national flag by the King of Prussia. Kings and princes yielded to popular demands by appointing liberal ministries, elections were held for representative assemblies, civic rights – especially freedom of the press – were proclaimed, and nationalist sentiment was given free rein. In Germany, a National Parliament met at Frankfurt to devise a constitution for a united Germany; in Hungary the Magyar leader, Kossuth, proclaimed Hungarian autonomy, and in Bohemia the Czechs convened a Slav Congress. In the Italian states, rulers hastily granted constitutions while in Lombardy and Venetia revolts broke out against Austrian rule.

However, the failure of the new regimes and governments to devise remedies for the hardships and grievances of the peasants and urban workers weakened the mass support which had made the revolutionary movements seem such a formidable force in the spring of 1848. [By the summer, the revolution was on the wane and by early 1849 many of the new assemblies had been dissolved and the new constitutions either abrogated or modified in the interests of the ruler.] The restoration of monarchical power and the influence of conservative élites was made possible by the weakness and indecisiveness of the new regimes and the loyalty of the armies to the traditional authorities, especially in Austria.

  * Despite all the upheavals and revolutionary excitement of 1848, no war broke out amongst the Great Powers. There were three main reasons for this. Firstly, both Britain and Russia exerted strong diplomatic influence to preserve peace. Secondly, Russia adopted a 'wait and see' policy towards the upheavals of 1848 which was explained the next year by Nesselrode on the grounds that 'non-intervention was the price Russia had to pay in order to keep France neutral'. Thirdly, although the leaders of the new republican regime in France felt obliged to make bold pronouncements, they also declared that 'the Republic will not start a war against anyone'. In the 'Manifesto to Europe' issued by Lamartine, the new Foreign Minister on 4 March 1848, France announced its recognition of the 1815 treaties, despite their lack of legality in the eyes of the Republic. In response, and with some prompting from Britain, the three eastern powers declared their pacific intentions towards France, providing she kept within her existing boundaries. Nevertheless, war involving at least two of the Great Powers seemed quite possible in 1848–9 over three issues: a Prussian crusade for Poland; the Danish–German dispute in the duchies of Schleswig-Holstein; and the liberation of Lombardy and Venetia from Austrian rule.

The idea of inciting a Polish uprising, with the promise of German support for a war to liberate Poland from Russian rule, originated from the deep hostility of German liberals towards autocratic Russia. The new liberal regime that came to power in Prussia in March 1848, with von Arnhim as Foreign Minister, also held the view that involvement in a foreign war would help to forge German unity. The policy was deeply flawed. Von Arnhim was wildly over-confident of Britain's benevolent neutrality and of French support for a crusade for Poland. Furthermore the Prussian King had no desire for a conflict with Russia. The discouraging response from the western powers obliged the Prussian liberals by late April to abandon the idea of liberating the Poles, and to seek to promote German unity by peaceful means.

* German nationalism also played a prominent part in the dispute over the Elbe Duchies, Schleswig and Holstein, whose rule by the Danish crown had been recognised by international agreement in the eighteenth century. Holstein, whose population was overwhelmingly German, was a member of the German Confederation, unlike Schleswig, which had a large Danish minority in the north. In 1848 the Estates of the duchies renounced the authority of the Danish King and appealed to the German Confederation and Prussia for aid. The Danish King, for his part, appealed to the Great Powers for support in resisting a violation of an international agreement. Britain, however, had no military force available, while neither Russia nor France regarded the issue as important enough to merit war with Prussia.

Palmerston, acting as mediator between the Danes and the Prussians, insisted on an armistice and succeeded in convincing the Prussians that they faced certain war with France and Russia if they did not desist. The success of Palmerston's diplomacy of bluff owed much to the attitude of the King of Prussia, who not only disliked being associated with the German liberals, but was also embarrassed by the Tsar's disapproval of his 'infamous' conduct in attacking another sovereign. Eventually, in 1849, Prussia agreed to a treaty based on a return to the status quo, which was subsequently confirmed at a five-power conference in London in 1851–2.

* The conflict in north Italy was complicated by the attempt of the

Piedmontese King to exploit the revolts against Austrian rule in Lombardy and Venetia to create a kingdom of north Italy with himself as king. That it did not result in a Franco-Austrian war was mainly due to the restraint, mingled with indecisiveness, shown by France when called upon for aid by Piedmont. The French government saw little advantage for France in a war whose main result would be the aggrandisement of Piedmont, whose recovery of Nice and Savoy in 1815 still rankled in France. After the defeat of the Piedmontese army by the Austrians in July 1848, the French succeeded in involving Britain in joint mediation, but long drawn out negotiations ended in deadlock. The issue was finally resolved when Piedmont renewed the war against Austria in March 1849, only to be beaten again within a week, leaving Austria in control of north Italy once more.

★ In 1849 the forces of 'order' reasserted themselves on the international scene: Austria defeated the Piedmontese army; France destroyed the short-lived Roman Republic in June and restored papal rule; and Russian forces assisted the Austrians in the suppression of the Hungarian rebellion between May and August. After the renewal of their revolution against Habsburg rule, the rebels had expelled the Austrian army in April 1849. But the Austrians had no reason to fear foreign intervention on behalf of the Hungarians. France was pursuing a conservative course in international affairs, while Britain regarded Austria's possession of Hungary as essential to her position as a Great Power. The Prussians promised military assistance in return for recognition of their supremacy in north Germany, while Russia offered military aid without strings attached. For Russia, the prospect of a Hungarian victory was alarming, lest the example should spread northwards into Galicia (Austrian Poland) and thence into Poland itself.

The Tsar, dubbed the 'gendarme of Europe', also presided over the fate of Germany in 1849–50. Both Austria and Prussia were exploring alternatives to restoring the German Confederation and promoted schemes for uniting the German states under their own leadership. Negotiations with other north German states for a limited German union under Prussia resulted in the creation of the Erfurt Union in May 1849. But the Austrian Chancellor, Schwarzenberg, insisted on reviving the old Diet of the Confederation. In 1850, a quarrel between the ruler and the Estates of Hesse raised in an acute form the issue of whether the old Confederation or the new Erfurt Union should exercise jurisdiction in the dispute. When the two German powers seemed on the brink of war in November 1850, neither France nor Britain would support Prussia, whose military action in Holstein had displeased them. Austria therefore held the trump diplomatic card – that of Russia's moral support. At Olmütz in November 1850, Prussia agreed to dissolve the Erfurt Union and to reconstitute the old German Confederation, thereby restoring Austria's ascendancy over Germany. Howeverer, the real victor was Russia, for whom a disunited Germany, with power shared between Austria and Prussia (so-called 'dualism'), was an ideal outcome. This marked the triumph of conservatism and reaction after the revolutions of 1848–9.

6 1815–48 – The 'Age of Metternich' and the Metternich 'System'?

In terms of continuity alone, as Chancellor of Austria and a leading European statesman from 1815 to 1848, there is a case for regarding the period from the Treaty of Vienna to the 1848 revolutions as the 'Age of Metternich'. Whether he consciously operated according to a 'system' is much less certain, but some historians believe there is sufficient coherence to Metternich's ideas ('principles' as he liked to call them) and consistency in their application to merit the use of the term.

Metternich's overriding objective was to defeat revolution and to maintain the existing international, political and social order. At the level of international politics, he wished to preserve the Vienna Settlement and the existing balance of power. In state politics, he was a fervent believer in monarchical government, combined with centralised bureaucratic rule. In social terms, he sought to maintain the dominance of the aristocracy and to keep the middle class at bay. This essentially static and conservative programme was to be achieved in three ways. Firstly, by the alliance of monarchical states committed to resisting revolution. Secondly, by means of efficient, paternalistic government which provided the benefits of education, justice and fair taxation for its subjects. Thirdly, the whole system was to be buttressed by a 'police' network, operating at the international level as well as within individual states.

It is generally agreed that whether or not there was a Metternich 'system', the Austrian Chancellor pursued policies that were based on fixed principles. Three of these were negative: hostility to revolution, liberalism and nationalism. To Metternich revolution was inherently evil and 'moderate' revolutions were a charade, since all revolutions contained an 'inner fatality' to proceed to extremes. For him they were the work of minorities who knew little of the world of politics. His hostility to liberalism stemmed from his view that individual liberty was simply an escape from authority, while constitutions were artificial creations: 'Men create Charters, time makes Constitutions'. As the chief minister of a multi-national state, he naturally believed that nationality was not the basis of society.

Metternich's fundamental belief was that monarchy was the only natural form of government, because the presence of a king at the head of the various layers of society provided a guarantee of social order. He did not advocate arbitrary or absolute monarchy, akin to dictatorship, since 'one does not govern with bayonets'. But the ruler was there to rule, to take advice and govern in an orderly fashion. Metternich despised constitutional monarchy on the British pattern, claiming that 'pure' monarchy was superior to it. His capacity for self-delusion is perhaps shown best by his pride in what he called 'dynamic conservatism', as opposed to reaction or immobilism. Stressing the benefits that paternalistic policies provided for the people, he insisted that real progress and change could only come from above. In 1847 he made this claim for the achievements of the Austrian Empire:

1 . . . everything there is progressing; everything that is good and useful is advancing . . . all the reasonable demands preached by the progressives have been fulfilled by us. Our Empire acknowledges the perfect equality of citizens before the law: we have no
5 tax privileges or feudal burdens; in our Empire is found equality of taxation and the independence of justice. All parts of the Empire have assemblies of estates and a municipal system much more liberal than that which exists in countries ruled by the modern representative system. In no other empire are the
10 nationalities more respected than ours; respect for the nationalities is indeed a necessary condition of our existence; nowhere is there less absolutist government than in our Empire, nor could there be any.

Metternich's main rival in the government, Count Kolowrat, did not take such a rosy view of the effect of his policies on the problems of the Empire. Addressing the Chancellor, he said:

1 I am an aristocrat by birth and by conviction and completely agree with you that people must strive for conservatism and do everything to achieve it. Yet we differ about means. Your means consist of a forest of bayonets and fixed adherence to things as
5 they are. To my mind, by following these lines we are playing into the hands of the revolutionaries . . . Your ways will lead us . . . not tomorrow or next year – but soon enough – to our ruin.

Despite Metternich's claim to be a 'dynamic conservative', in practice he almost always seemed to have a reason why changes should not be made. This point, together with the dangers of ignoring demands for reform, was emphasised in Palmerston's comments to the Austrian ambassador in London:

1 Prince Metternich believes that he is a conservative by obstinately upholding the political status quo in Europe: we believe that we are conservatives by everywhere preaching and counselling reforms and improvements where these things are designated and
5 claimed to be necessary by the public. You, on the other hand, reject everything. When order and tranquillity reign in your land,

you say that concessions are useless; in moments of crisis and
revolt you equally refuse them, not wishing to weaken authority
by appearing to bend before the storm. You also persist in
10 rejecting absolutely everything that public opinion demands in
your country and in the lands in which you have influence and
patronage . . . No, this immobility is not conservatism . . . Your
repressive and suffocating policy is also a fatal one and will lead to
an explosion just as certainly as would a boiler that was hermeti-
15 cally sealed and deprived of an outlet for steam.

Metternich's 'system' can be seen in operation through his control
over 'police' activities, his influence over Germany and his direction of
policy in north Italy and Hungary. The main objective, of course, was
to prevent or suppress revolutions but in Italy and Hungary his
doctrinaire belief in bureaucratic centralisation was also evident.
Metternich's Chancellery in Vienna was the centre of a vast information
network, employing the services of political police and agents, who sent
regular reports to Vienna, infiltrated secret societies and engaged in
various other 'cloak and dagger' activities. Postal treaties with other
states provided opportunities for Austrian officials to interfere with
private correspondence. A Central Information Commission was set up
in Germany to coordinate the supervision of subversive activities, but
not in Italy where the rulers were resentful of too much Austrian
interference. The Italian states also rejected Metternich's plan for an
Italian League, to create the sort of centralised direction over political
affairs that was provided by the Confederation in Germany.
  An essential element in Metternich's system was the assertion of
Austrian influence over Germany and, if possible, the direction of
Prussian policy. Metternich succeeded in discouraging the Prussian
King from honouring his pledges, made in 1813, to grant a constitution
which would have strengthened Prussia's claims to leadership of
liberal–nationalist opinion in Germany. By 1820, Prussia had become a
docile follower of Austrian foreign policy. The German Confederation
set up in 1815 proved to be a valuable means of exercising control over
the German states. Metternich was astute enough to consult with
Prussia about German affairs so that no open disagreements arose
between the two powers. The business of the Diet was 'fixed' in such a
way that Austro-Prussian dominance was assured, especially when the
rulers took fright at signs of unrest.
  The assassination of a reactionary writer and journalist, Kotzebue
(allegedly a Tsarist agent) in March 1819 presented Metternich with a
perfect excuse for repressive measures. Since the murder was the work
of a nationalistic student organisation, the *Burschenschaft*, it was
possible to introduce the Carlsbad Decrees, passed by the Diet in
September 1819, to tighten control over the universities, student
societies and the press. The crisis was also exploited to amend Article

XIII of the 1815 constitution of the Confederation which stated: 'Each state will create a constitution based on assemblies'. The whole episode was a remarkable demonstration of Metternich's ascendancy over the German states, whose rulers welcomed him as a saviour from the dreaded revolution. Disturbances in the early 1830s led to the Six Acts being passed by the Diet in 1832 closing universities, tightening censorship and intensifying surveillance of 'subversives'.

Metternich's control over policy towards the Italian and Hungarian kingdoms enabled him to centralise much of the administration of these two parts of the Empire, so that important decisions were taken in Vienna. In Lombardy and Venetia the Viceroy and the diets had no real power, increasing the feeling of Italians that they were subjected to 'alien' rule. On the other hand, the provinces were the best-governed states in Italy and their flourishing economies produced higher living standards than in any of the states governed by Italian rulers. Although it may be said that it was no fault of Metternich's that his advice to reform their administrations was ignored, in another sense it shows the limitations of Metternich's system. Being able to count on Austrian aid to suppress a revolt against misgovernment removed the most powerful incentive for despots, such as the King of Naples, to mend their ways.

Metternich's determination to assert centralised rule from Vienna was clearly shown in his hostility towards representative institutions in Hungary, where public opinion was still a force. The main objects of his attack, apart from the liberal Hungarian reform movement, were the Diet and the elective system of county administration. Their influence was reduced by resorting to unscrupulous methods. Pressure was exercised on voters, the press was muzzled, prominent politicians were charged with treason and the secret police were widely employed. In the 1840s Metternich proposed to replace elected county administrators by officials appointed by Vienna and to overawe opposition in the Diet by empowering the police to attend its sessions. He was even prepared to risk a national uprising to achieve these aims but, in the event, it was not until after his dismissal in March 1848 that the Hungarian revolution broke out.

Some historians have argued that Metternich's philosophy was little more than a rationalisation of Austria's needs. The case for this is quite strong. While liberalism would weaken the Emperor's authority, nationalism would lead to the disintegration of the Empire. Secondly, his ideal system of government bore little relation to the realities of political life under the Habsburg emperors of this period. While Francis I (1792–1835) was averse to working in an organised fashion, his successor, Ferdinand (1835–48) was quite unfit to govern at all! Thirdly, Austria suffered from grave financial and, consequently, military weaknesses. To balance the budget, expenditure on the army had to be cut and her military weakness was a serious limitation on an active foreign policy. To conceal Austria's weakness, Metternich adopted a strategy at the international level of persuading the Great Powers to act in concert to check those forces which threatened the stability and survival of the Austrian Empire.

Metternich's 'system' had to be a European system because of the Austrian Empire's vulnerability to the challenge of liberal and nationalist ideas. It was therefore thought to be essential to check the spread of these ideas in Europe as a whole, especially in Italy and Germany. Another factor was that Austria was actually too weak to be a Great Power unless she could rely on the support of other powers. Hence the desire to make Prussian policy subordinate to Austria's needs and the necessity of steering Russian policy along the path of conservatism, especially after the decline of the entente with Britain in 1820. Austria's very survival seemed to require the maintenance of peace and order throughout Europe and the continuance of the balance of power.

In seeking to impose his system on Europe, Metternich's task was facilitated by the 1815 settlement and his ability to appeal to the sanctity of treaties when events threatened it. The series of congresses held between 1815 and 1822 also provided him with opportunities to convince other statesmen, especially Alexander, that there really was a revolutionary conspiracy in Europe, which he succeeded in doing in 1820 at the Congress of Troppau. Metternich's influence over Russia was shown again in 1833, when the Tsar, Nicholas I, agreed to concerted action against threats to the monarchical principle.

Perhaps the term 'system' is too mechanical for the adroit manoeuvring that Metternich excelled in. A better description of his work might be that he devised a broad political strategy which he pursued with considerable consistency. The merits of his strategy and his degree of success in pursuing it have long been matters of debate. Metternich's critics believe he showed excessive anxiety over manifestations of moderate liberal views, and by inhibiting gradual, orderly change he contributed to the very explosion he sought to prevent – the revolutionary upheavals of 1848. In particular, Paul Schroeder has suggested that his 'Europeanism' was just a smoke screen for Austrian self interest, while A. J. P. Taylor has derided Metternich's 'principles' as clichés containing less profundity than the ideas most men have when shaving! In the view of his critics, Metternich's attitudes were too negative, his approach too doctrinaire, for a great statesman.

On the other hand, Metternich's defence of the conservative order in Europe has been admired by other writers from the classic work of von Srbik (1925) to the study by Henry Kissinger over 30 years later. Central to the defence of Metternich's diplomacy is the belief that Austria, despite her weakness, was a 'European necessity'. Her key role in European affairs was as a bulwark of stability and order in central and eastern Europe – a role expanded by some (especially American) historians in the 1950s to include the defence of western civilisation against the threat from the east. Metternich's success in winning Russia

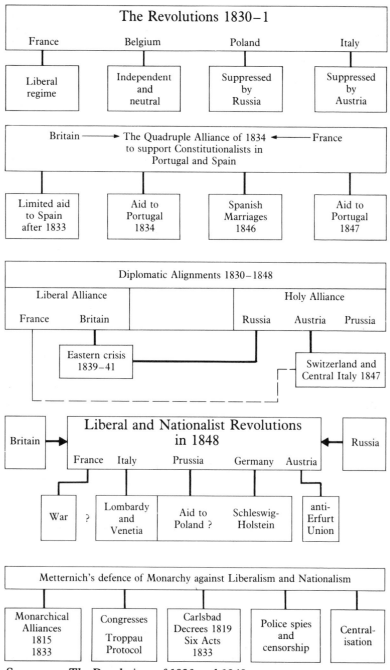

The Revolutions 1830–1

France	Belgium	Poland	Italy
Liberal regime	Independent and neutral	Suppressed by Russia	Suppressed by Austria

Britain ⟶ The Quadruple Alliance of 1834 ⟵ France
to support Constitutionalists in
Portugal and Spain

Limited aid to Spain after 1833	Aid to Portugal 1834	Spanish Marriages 1846	Aid to Portugal 1847

Diplomatic Alignments 1830–1848

Liberal Alliance		Holy Alliance		
France Britain		Russia Austria Prussia		

Eastern crisis 1839–41

Switzerland and Central Italy 1847

Liberal and Nationalist Revolutions in 1848

Britain ⟶   ⟵ Russia

France	Italy	Prussia	Germany	Austria
War	?	Lombardy and Venetia	Aid to Poland ?	Schleswig-Holstein

anti-Erfurt Union

Metternich's defence of Monarchy against Liberalism and Nationalism

Monarchical Alliances 1815 1833	Congresses Troppau Protocol	Carlsbad Decrees 1819 Six Acts 1833	Police spies and censorship	Central-isation

Summary – The Revolutions of 1830 and 1848

to the cause of peace and conservatism cannot be denied and the solidarity of the three eastern powers after the Münchengrätz and Berlin agreements was certainly a significant factor in international affairs from 1833 to 1848.

The 'Age of Metternich' can therefore be regarded as, in some ways, a useful shorthand description of the period 1815 to 1848, though it might be questioned whether his influence was as great after 1830 as it had been before that date. It is hard to deny that for much of the period 1815 to 1848 most of Europe more closely resembled Metternich's ideals than those of his opponents. In addition, he exercised a powerful influence over European diplomacy for over 30 years, but in a less creative way than either Castlereagh or Palmerston, his diplomatic rival after 1830. In international affairs there were also two noticeable limitations to Metternich's influence. Firstly, the affairs of western Europe and, in particular, the fate of Belgium and the Iberian Peninsula, were decided mainly by Britain and France. Secondly, it was Russia and Britain who largely determined the outcome of the Eastern Question from 1815 to 1848.

Making notes on 'The Revolutions of 1830 and 1848'

Once again, detailed notes will be required on most of this chapter. But an added complication is that you must prepare yourself to use the factual content of the chapter in a number of different ways, by putting it together in a wide variety of combinations. You would therefore be well advised to separate out the facts from the historical issues to be considered and to note them separately.

The facts. Skim read the chapter picking out the facts by stopping each time you come across a date. For each dated event (or group of them if they are within the same section of sub-section) note down what happened. Be as brief as possible. It will greatly aid your understanding (as well as providing a useful summary for revision) if you compile a list of the facts you have noted. The list should be in chronological order, thus becoming a date chart. In each case, only include the date and a name for the event, so that each event fits on a single line.

The historical issues. Write brief answers to the following questions. The numbers refer to the section of the chapter in which the answer is to be found.

1.   What was 'Conference Diplomacy'?
2a).   What was the effect of the revolution of 1830 in France on international relations?
2b)/c). Why was there no war between the Great Powers in the 1830s over the Belgian, Polish and Italian revolts?

3/4.   Why did the Quadruple Alliance not form an effective counterbalance to the Holy Alliance?

6.   What were Metternich's aims in international affairs? What methods did he use in his attempt to achieve them?

Source-based questions on 'The Revolutions of 1830 and 1848'

1 Metternich

Carefully read the extracts from Metternich's letter to the Austrian ambassador in Rome, Kolowrat's statement and Palmerston's comments, given on pages 72–3. Answer the following questions.

a) What is meant by 'feudal burdens' in the first extract, 'a forest of bayonets' in the second extract, and 'designated and claimed to be necessary by the public' in the third extract? (6 marks)

b) What main argument does Metternich use to defend his policy? (2 marks)

c) What flaws are there in Metternich's argument? (5 marks)

d) What are the similarities between the criticisms of Metternich made by Kolowrat and by Palmerston? (3 marks)

e) On what do Metternich, Kolowrat and Palmerston agree? (4 marks)

CHAPTER 5

The Great Powers and the Eastern Question 1821–56

1 The Eastern Question

The Eastern Question – the problem of what to do about the decline and possible disintegration of the Ottoman Empire – was a recurring issue in international affairs throughout the nineteenth century. Turkey's decline had important, though different, implications for most of the Great Powers individually, as well as serious repercussions on the relations between them. The Eastern Question was therefore a major challenge to the Great Powers acting collectively as the Concert of Europe. The fate of the Turkish Empire became a source of rivalry and suspicion among the major European states because they were unable to agree on a 'solution' to the problem posed by Turkey's decline. In the absence of any such agreement, the Eastern Question took the form of a series of crises which culminated, in this period, in the Crimean War of 1854–6.

By the early nineteenth century, the Ottoman Empire had already become a ramshackle state, a pale shadow of its former power and glory in the sixteenth century. The Turkish government at Constantinople (modern Istanbul), commonly referred to by European governments as 'the Porte' – a name derived from the Grand Vizier's palace, the 'Sublime Porte' – certainly had many problems to contend with. The Sultan claimed some sort of authority over territories extending from the borders of Austria and Russia through the Balkans and Asia Minor to Persia, through Syria and Palestine to parts of Arabia, as well as Egypt and the coast of North Africa (see map on page 80). Governing such a vast empire, which contained so many different nationalities and religions, was clearly a daunting task – even with the system of devolving power to local notables and chieftains, as in the case of the pashaliks of Egypt and Syria. Effective government ultimately depended on energetic and resourceful direction from Constantinople, which many of the Sultans of this period were incapable of providing.

To westerners, the most obvious feature of Turkey's decline was her military weakness. This had been demonstrated in dramatic form by Russia's spectacular victories over Turkey in the war of 1768–74. The Janissaries, whose former military prowess had twice made Vienna the outpost of Christian Europe's defences against the spread of militant Islam, had degenerated into a rabble by 1815. Although still a privileged caste, they were untrained and undisciplined, posing a greater threat to the Sultan's subjects than to his enemies abroad until their suppression in 1826. The causes of Turkey's military and political decline are not altogether clear. Some European historians stress the

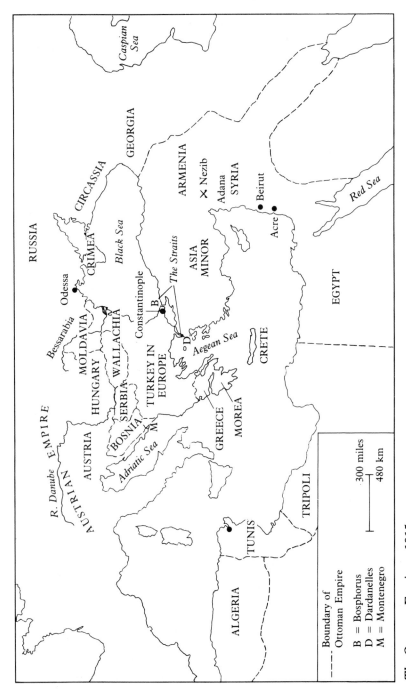

The Ottoman Empire c. 1815

RUSSIA

Caspian Sea

GEORGIA

CIRCASSIA

ARMENIA

✕ Nezib

Adana

SYRIA

● Beirut

● Acre

Red Sea

CRIMEA

Black Sea

Odessa ●

Bessarabia

MOLDAVIA

The Straits

ASIA MINOR

EGYPT

HUNGARY

WALLACHIA

Constantinople

B ●

○ D

Aegean Sea

R. Danube   EMPIRE

SERBIA

TURKEY IN EUROPE

CRETE

AUSTRIAN

AUSTRIA

BOSNIA

M

Adriatic Sea

GREECE

MOREA

TRIPOLI

● TUNIS

ALGERIA

- - - Boundary of
       Ottoman Empire

B = Bosphorus
D = Dardanelles
M = Montenegro

300 miles

480 km

importance of intellectual stagnation and regression, caused by the opposition of privileged groups (especially religious leaders and teachers) to adaptation and change proposed by reforming ministers. As a result, nineteenth-century Turkey suffered the disadvantages of 'a medieval mentality and a medieval economy' while trying to support a large, but inefficient army and bureaucracy.

Despite these obstacles, some reforms did take place, including military and naval modernisation carried out under European experts and advisers. Such measures, albeit sporadic and incomplete, contributed to the ability of the Ottoman Empire to survive into the twentieth century, despite frequent unrest and the encroachment of her more powerful European neighbours. Nevertheless, it seems clear that the survival of the Empire down to 1914 depended less on her own efforts than on the attitude of the European powers towards her. If, for example, the Great Powers had been able to agree on a scheme of partition, as suggested at different times by Russia and Germany, Turkey could scarcely have avoided being reduced to something like its present size, with its 'heartland' in Asia Minor. In the event, several of the Great Powers saw some advantage to themselves in the preservation of this weak, if unstable state, despite its sometimes barbaric treatment of the Christian population of European Turkey.

a) The Interests of the Great Powers

Of all the Great Powers, Russia was the one most directly involved in the fate of the Ottoman Empire. As a result of a series of successful wars against the Turks from 1768 to 1812, Russia had pushed her boundaries southwards to reach the northern shores of the Black Sea. Further to the east, she had also made gains in the northern Caucasus which, although causing less alarm to the western powers, were an important aspect of Russia's expansionist designs on the Ottoman Empire. Her military successes brought her more than territorial gain. By the Treaty of Kutchuk-Kainardji of 1774, she acquired three important rights. One of these was freedom of navigation for Russian merchant shipping in the Black Sea – hitherto a 'Turkish lake'. The second was the right of passage for merchantmen through the Straits (the Bosphorous and Dardanelles) into the Mediterranean. The third was an ill-defined right of protection over the Orthodox Church which, 75 years later, was to be greatly exaggerated by the Russian government. The very limited nature of the religious concession granted in 1774 is shown in this extract from the treaty:

1 *Art VII.* The Sublime Porte promises to protect constantly the Christian religion and its churches, and it also allows the Minister of the Imperial Court of Russia to make, upon all occasions, representations, as well in favour of the new church at Constanti-

5 nople, of which mention will be made in Article XIV, as on behalf
of its officiating ministers, promising to take such representations
into consideration, as being made by a confidential functionary of
a neighbouring and sincerely friendly Power . . .
Art XIV. After the manner of the other Powers, permission is
10 given to the High Court of Russia . . . to erect . . . a public church
of the Greek ritual, which shall always be under the protection of
the Ministers of that Empire, and secure from all coercion and
outrage . . .
Art XVI. The Empire of Russia restores to the Sublime Porte the
15 whole of Bessarabia . . . and the two Principalities of Wallachia
and Moldavia . . . and the Sublime Porte receives them upon the
following conditions, solemnly promising to keep them re-
ligiously . . .
. . . To obstruct in no manner whatsoever the free exercise of the
20 Christian religion, and to interpose no obstacle to the erection of
new churches and to the repairing of the old ones, as has been
done heretofore . . .

The maritime rights granted by this treaty were of great importance
to Russia's economic development in the nineteenth century, especially
with regard to her grain exports to Europe. It therefore became a
maxim of Russian policy that Constantinople and the Straits must
either remain in Turkish hands or, failing that, come under Russian
control. If they were allowed to fall into the hands of another power,
Russia might suffer economic strangulation.

After 1815, Russia did not consistently hold the expansionist designs
on the Turkish Empire attributed to her by the other Great Powers. It
was more a case of choosing between several options, at different times.
One option was, indeed, to seek further territorial gains at Turkey's
expense in Asia Minor or in the Balkans (Turkey in Europe). Alterna-
tively, Russia could support the efforts of her fellow Slavs in the
Balkans to throw off Turkish rule. A second option, and one favoured
by an influential group amongst the Tsar's advisers, was to seek to
preserve Turkey in her existing condition of gradual decline. This had
the advantage for Russia that Turkey was a weak neighbour which
posed no threat to her, which was preferable to having a stronger state
(such as Austria) bordering on Russia in its place. However, an
essential condition of this policy of restraint towards Turkey was that
Russian influence should be predominant at Constantinople.

The Austrian Empire was the only other Great Power whose territory
bordered on Turkey in Europe. In 1815, Austria's main preoccupations
lay in central and western Europe, so she had no serious designs on
Turkish territory in this period. In general, the Austrians regarded the
Ottoman Empire as a useful bulwark against further Russian expansion
and therefore sought to preserve, not weaken it. In addition, they did

not share Russia's sympathy for the stirrings of Slav nationalist feeling in the Balkans, for fear of the effect of it on their own Slav peoples.

By the mid-nineteenth century, Britain had committed herself to the preservation of the Ottoman Empire. However, in the early 1800s there had been little to suggest that Britain would adopt such a role – the strong protest at Russia's gains from Turkey in 1790 was a temporary aberration. After all, in the 1820s, Britain supported the Greeks in their struggle for independence from the Turks. The key factor in the change of British policy was, unquestionably, suspicion of Russia's aims, although these fears were sometimes exaggerated. Britain's main anxiety was that control of Constantinople by Russia would lead to a marked growth in Russian power in the eastern Mediterranean. Such an event would enable her to extend her influence throughout the Near East and Middle East, including Egypt, carrying a threat to communications with India. Another factor that explains British concern for the stability and survival of the Ottoman Empire was the steady growth of Britain's trade and investments in Turkey after 1815, which might suffer substantially from uncertainty about her fate.

Nevertheless, an influential body of opinion in Britain deplored the whole idea of supporting what a British minister in 1830 called 'this clumsy fabric of barbarous power'. Consequently, British policy towards Turkey and, by extension, the government's attitude towards Russia's presumed designs on her, was liable to fluctuate according to which party or political group was in power. At the level of personalities, Palmerston spoke for the anti-Russian faction while Aberdeen represented the anti-Turk lobby. Another complicating factor was British public opinion. This could, on occasion, be aroused by the press to a frenzy of either anti-Russian or anti-Turkish feeling – mainly the former in this period.

France's political and commercial links with Turkey went back over several centuries. The system of 'Capitulations', by which Europeans enjoyed special privileges (including immunity from Turkish law) had been developed for France's benefit. The King of France had been recognised as the protector of the interests of the Catholic Church in the Sultan's dominions. Consequently, France enjoyed considerable diplomatic influence at Constantinople in this period from her historic links with the Porte. This influence, however, had been temporarily put in jeopardy by Napoleon's expedition to Egypt in 1798–9, which had greatly offended the Sultan. On the other hand, French influence in Egypt was considerably enhanced by such links and led to France treating the Pasha of Egypt, Mehemet Ali, as her protégé in the 1830s. It was natural for France, with her major commercial port of Marseilles and naval base at Toulon, to regard the Mediterranean as an area for extending French influence – regardless of the resultant rivalry with Britain. However, her military expedition to Algiers in 1830 was an impulsive move, out of keeping with her usual strategy of extending

French influence gradually through trade, finance, and technical assistance as, for example, was the case in Egypt.

The power with the least involvement or interest in Turkish affairs in this period was Prussia. Even so, she could not entirely dissociate herself from the Eastern Question. Apart from the obligation, as one of the five Great Powers of Europe, to play a role in such an important issue in international affairs, she was linked by the 'Holy Alliance' to both Austria and Russia, who were deeply involved in the Eastern Question. Lacking the strength or self-confidence to act as mediator between her two allies, Prussia tended to follow Vienna's lead, but with many an anxious glance in the direction of St Petersburg.

2 The Greek Revolt, 1821–31

The Greek revolt hardly lived up to the romantics' ideal of a heroic struggle for national independence, personified by the tragic death in a noble cause of the poet Byron at Missolonghi in 1824. Instead, it was a bloody and prolonged affair, spread over nine years, during which both sides slaughtered each other mercilessly and the Greeks frequently fell out among themselves.

The main areas of the fighting were the Morea and the Greek islands of the Aegean (see map on page 92). The Revolutionary and Napoleonic wars had provided many Greeks with military and naval experience. At the same time, French ideals had fired the expanding middle class – enriched by the growth of sea-borne trade with the Russian port of Odessa – with the idea of liberation from Turkish rule. By 1824 the Greeks seemed to have gained the upper hand, but their success prompted the Sultan to appeal for aid from his vassal Mehemet Ali, an Albanian adventurer, now Pasha of Egypt. Egyptian intervention in 1824–5 tipped the scales against the Greeks, whose cause was also weakened by internal rivalries. By 1825–6 it was clear that unless the European powers intervened the Greek revolt would be suppressed.

Although Mehemet Ali had some sympathisers in France, public opinion in general (in both France and Britain) was on the side of the Greeks who were, somewhat simplistically, regarded as the heirs and custodians of the glories of Ancient Greece. In Russia, opinion focused more on the fate of their co-religionists, the Greek branch of the Orthodox Church. Despite this, until 1825–6 European intervention seemed unlikely.

The initial reaction of the Great Powers to the Greek revolt had been distinctly cool, as shown by their condemnation of it in 1822 at the Congress of Verona as 'a rash and criminal enterprise'. Metternich naturally attacked the uprising in Greece as another manifestation of the revolutionary spirit that threatened monarchical rule in Europe and sought to persuade the Tsar that he should not aid these rebels against their legitimate ruler, the Sultan. In order to deprive Russia of an excuse for war with Turkey, Britain joined Austria in putting pressure on the Porte to reduce Russian dissatisfaction by meeting her legitimate grievances over the non-fulfilment of the Treaty of Bucharest of 1812. Nevertheless, the Greek revolt continued to trouble the Great Powers for several years. The failure of the Turks to suppress it quickly allowed time for the Tsar to be subjected to mounting pressure from within Russia to intervene on the Greeks' behalf. Although he was reluctant to act unilaterally against Turkey, Alexander became impatient at the obstructive attitude of the other powers to his attempts to secure a solution to the problem through congresses in St Petersburg in 1824–5. This stemmed from Metternich's persistent refusal to agree to aiding a revolt, while Canning suspected Russia, not unjustly, of attempting to use it to undermine Turkey by setting up weak client states under Russian influence.

The deadlock was broken by Canning's change of front in 1826. He decided that it was better to cooperate with Russia in order to restrain her, than to persist in opposing her and risk unilateral Russian action. His decision was also influenced by pressure from public opinion to stop the wholesale massacre of the Greeks by the Egyptian forces. Britain and Russia agreed, in the St Petersburg Protocol of April 1826, on setting up an autonomous Greek state under Turkish suzerainty. A loosely-worded clause also permitted intervention by either or both powers if it became necessary to use force to prevent the revolt from being suppressed. The assumption behind this Anglo-Russian agreement, to which France adhered in July 1827, was that the revolt could be brought to an end by the mediation of the three powers at Constantinople. When the Sultan rejected their offer of mediation, the three powers were left with no clearly agreed policy on what to do next.

Fate intervened in the person of Admiral Codrington, commander of the British squadron of the allied fleet which was blockading the Morea to prevent supplies reaching the Turco-Egyptian forces by sea. On entering Navarino Bay in October 1827, the British squadron was fired upon. Codrington's instructions did not cover such an eventuality. In an excess of zeal, he opened fire on his attackers and promptly sank the Turco-Egyptian fleet – 'an untoward event', as the British Prime Minister laconically observed!

Navarino had important effects on the situation. Firstly, the Sultan proclaimed a 'holy war' against Russia, regarded as the instigator of the hostile blockade. Secondly, the Turks (not surprisingly) became even more intransigent in their attitude towards the efforts of the three powers to mediate in the Greek conflict. Thirdly, the British government, embarrassed by Codrington's drastic action, became reluctant to approve any further measures against the Turks. Consequently, it was left to France to send troops to evict the Egyptians from the Morea, while Russia provided funds and supplies for the Greek forces. In actual fact, the Greeks benefited more from the distraction of Turkey's war with Russia. Russia had declared war on Turkey in April 1828, after the Sultan had denounced a recent agreement on the administration of the Danubian principalities (modern Rumania). After a sluggish campaign in the principalities in 1828, one Russian army reached Adrianople, less than 150 miles from Constantinople, in August 1829, while another army was advancing in the Caucasus. The Sultan then sued for peace. In the Treaty of Adrianople of September 1829, the Russians sought only modest rewards in Turkey in Europe, but made substantial gains in Asia Minor, including two Black Sea ports and recognition of their claims to Georgia and Armenia.

Turkey's defeat by Russia severely weakened her ability to resist pressure to discuss the terms for a settlement of the Greek revolt. After prolonged and difficult negotiations in London from 1829 to 1831 the representatives of the three powers eventually agreed on the frontiers of Greece and its status as an independent monarchy, under the rule of a European prince. Although the kingdom of Greece gained more than the mere autonomy which had originally been proposed, Britain and France insisted on limiting the size of the new state, for fear that it would become a Russian satellite.

The solution of the Greek revolt without a conflict among the Great Powers has been called 'a major illustration and accomplishment of the Concert of Europe'. However, it was not a triumph for the Congress System, which had clearly failed to cope with the divergence of views among the five Great Powers, especially the persistent Austro-Prussian refusal to countenance support for rebels. It was primarily their rigidity that made the congresses of 1824–5 in St Petersburg abortive. The British decision, followed by that of France, to try to work with Russia rather than against her, provided the element of flexibility needed for successful cooperation by the Great Powers. In this sense 'Conference Diplomacy', securing as much consensus as was possible in a given situation, was a necessary substitute for the over-rigid Congress System which had become an impediment to the successful operation of the Concert of Europe.

3 The Great Powers and Mehemet Ali

a) The Crisis of 1831–3

On two occasions in the 1830s the survival of the Ottoman Empire seemed to be at risk. The unusual feature of this period of the Eastern Question was that the threat came not from Russia, but from the Sultan's own vassal, Mehemet Ali, Pasha of Egypt. The military ineptitude of the Sultan's armies twice left Constantinople open to the Pasha's superior forces. Whether Mehemet Ali would actually have taken advantage of the opportunity to overthrow the Sultan if the powers had not intervened, is not altogether clear. It is difficult to gauge the real extent of his ambitions, which were affected by his grievance over the Sultan's refusal to grant him Syria, as well as Crete, in return for his aid against the Greeks. He was certainly determined to secure Syria, which was occupied by Egyptian forces in 1831–2. By February 1833 these forces had advanced to within 150 miles of Constantinople, prompting the Sultan to appeal to the European powers for aid.

Although all the Great Powers were concerned at the threat to the Sultan's regime, Russia was far and away the most alarmed by Ali's challenge. The explanation of this apparent *volte face* in Russia's attitude towards the Sultan's authority lies in the report of a special committee set up by the Tsar in 1829 to examine Russo-Turkish relations. The Kochubei Committee (named after its chairman) concluded that the advantages for Russia of preserving the Ottoman Empire far outweighed the disadvantages. Turkey's weakness made her a relatively harmless neighbour and Russia had no desire for further expansion at this period. The destruction of Turkey in Europe, on the other hand, could well result in territorial gains by Russia's rivals. Furthermore, the contraction of the Sultan's authority to Asia Minor might result in the emergence of a strong, ethnically homogeneous Turkish state, which would be more capable of resisting Russia in the Caucasus. In approving this analysis, the Tsar emphasised that major territorial changes could only be considered in the context of an international agreement. This cautious, conservative approach remained the basis of Russian policy towards Turkey for the next 20 years, albeit with the objective of 'maintaining Turkey in the stagnant state it finds itself in'.

It was, therefore, not in Russia's interest in 1833 to see the Sultan's rule overthrown and probably replaced by a more vigorous regime under Mehemet Ali. Since Ali was regarded as a protégé of France, his triumph would serve to increase French influence in the Near and Middle East, to the detriment of Russia. Furthermore, Ali was in rebellion against his legitimate suzerain, and Nicholas' fear of revolution had recently been intensified by the overthrow of the Bourbon monarchy in France. There were very sound reasons, therefore, why Russia – Turkey's most dangerous adversary for the previous 60 years – should take the seemingly bizarre step of offering the Sultan military assistance for the defence of Constantinople. Consequently, in February 1833, a Russian squadron arrived off the Bosphorus, followed some weeks later by several thousand Russian troops. Despite its somewhat belated arrival, this show of force (combined with pressure from the other powers) induced Mehemet Ali to come to terms with the Sultan. By May 1833 he had secured recognition of his claim to rule Syria, with the northern district of Adana for his son, Ibrahim, the very able commander of his forces.

Russia's reward for her aid was the Treaty of Unkiar-Skelessi (July

1833). Ostensibly a treaty of mutual defence, its real significance lay in its secret clauses. In them, Russia waived her right to Turkish aid, if attacked by another state, in return for the closure of the Straits to all warships (Russian included) 'not allowing any foreign vessels to enter the Straits on any pretext whatever'. Despite the fact that the closure of the Straits to warships while Turkey was at peace was already an ancient rule, the Russians regarded this secret clause as an additional guarantee of the security of their Black Sea coast. They also believed that in any future crisis the Turks would turn to Russia first for support which signified, the Russian Foreign Minister claimed, that 'our intervention in the affairs of Turkey has acquired a basis of legality'.

If the other Great Powers, especially Britain and France, were so concerned at the outcome of Russian intervention in 1833, this raises the question why they had not responded to the Sultan's appeal for aid. After all, it was only after his appeal to the western powers had been rejected that Turkey had turned to Russia – a dangerous course which a Turkish minister justified on the grounds that 'a drowning man will clutch at a serpent'.

Britain's inaction during the crisis of 1831–3 was the product of two factors. Firstly, Palmerston did press for British support for the Sultan but he was overruled by the Cabinet, on the grounds that the active British fleet was fully committed off the coasts of Holland and Portugal. To provide a squadron for action in the Near East would necessitate asking Parliament for extra funds which the government was reluctant to do, for fear of being attacked by the opposition over it. In the acrimonious state of British party politics at this time, with a general election in the offing, the Whig government decided not to risk its popularity for the Sultan's sake. The second factor was simply that some influential members of the Cabinet believed that the Ottoman Empire was beyond redemption and should be left to its fate.

The attitude of France to the problem was complicated by her desire to preserve Mehemet Ali as an agent of French influence in the Mediterranean. Consequently, rather than offer direct aid to Turkey, she preferred to work for a compromise settlement between the Sultan and Ali that would avoid the need for military intervention by the powers.

Austria's response to the crisis had been to propose concerted action by the Great Powers but this did not materialise. Afterwards, her anxiety about the real aims of Russian policy was relieved by her agreement with Russia at Münchengrätz in September 1833, which restored the unity of purpose of the Holy Alliance. Austria was assured of Russia's desire to preserve the Ottoman Empire and of her willingness to concert with Austria if its collapse seemed inevitable. Both powers also agreed on the need to defend the Sultan against any future threat from Mehemet Ali.

The main effect of the crisis of 1831–3 on international relations was to deepen British and French mistrust of Russian policy in the Near East. In particular, the quite mistaken belief that Russia had secured an exclusive right of passage for her warships through the Straits created great alarm. The Treaty of Unkiar-Skelessi was generally regarded by other European states as almost reducing Turkey to the status of a Russian protectorate – 'taking the place by sap rather than by storm', as Palmerston put it. Although this was an exaggerated view, Britain and France, unlike Austria, had to wait until 1839 for positive proof that Russia wished to act in concert with the other powers in the Eastern Question. In the next crisis in 1839, Palmerston was determined to undo the advantages which he believed Russia had derived from her aid to the Sultan in 1833.

b) The Crisis of 1839–41

The renewal of the crisis in the Near East in 1839 arose from the Sultan's desire for revenge against Mehemet Ali. Confident of success following the reorganisation of the Turkish army since 1833, the Sultan ordered the invasion of Syria in May 1839. However, his forces were routed by the Egyptians at the battle of Nezib in June, leaving Constantinople open to attack – especially after the desertion of the Turkish fleet to the Egyptian side and the sudden death of the Sultan. Once again Turkey was saved by European intervention, but with some important differences from the earlier crisis in 1833. The Great Powers seemed agreed on resolving the crisis of 1839 by collective action, as opposed to unilateral action by Russia. In 1840, however, a serious confrontation developed between France and Britain, with the result that Britain depended on Russia's cooperation to resolve the dispute with Ali.

The initial response of the Great Powers to the Turkish defeat in 1839 was to assure the new Sultan of their collective support. This was intended to deter him from making sweeping concessions to Mehemet Ali. The united front of the Great Powers, which owed something to Metternich's initiative in summoning a conference at Vienna, broke down dramatically in the spring of 1840. Thiers, the new French Prime Minister, openly sided with Ali, with the aim of extracting generous concessions from the new Sultan as a way of resolving the crisis. Although France was entitled to seek to increase her influence in the Levant (the eastern Mediterranean) by pursuing a bold policy of her own, her action threatened to destroy the European Concert. It also carried the risk of humiliation for France if the other Great Powers closed ranks against her.

Thier's policy provided the Tsar with the opportunity he had been seeking since late 1839 to drive a wedge between the Liberal Alliance partners. Russia's policy of close cooperation with Britain enabled Palmerston to ride roughshod over the French, ignoring their support for Ali, and facilitated his triumph over his critics in the British Cabinet. The fate of Mehemet Ali, and of Thiers' policy, was virtually sealed by the Treaty of London in July 1840. By this treaty, from which France was excluded, the other Great Powers agreed on an ultimatum to Ali and authorised military action to coerce him, if he rejected the terms offered. France reacted to this treaty with belligerent threats, directed partly against Britain, which was not surprising. What was rather odd was the threat to unleash a war on the Rhine. After all, invading Germany was not a very appropriate retaliation for the humiliating failure of her policy in the Levant. The diplomatic tension ended in October with the dismissal of Thiers by the King, who indicated France's willingness to rejoin the European Concert even though military action was continuing against the Egyptians.

Mehemet Ali's rejection of those terms of the Treaty of London which applied to him – hereditary rule over Egypt and the pashalik of southern Syria for his lifetime – obliged the powers to enforce his submission to the Sultan. A British squadron bombarded Beirut in September and landed Turkish troops there. This was followed in November by the bombardment and capture of Acre. By February 1841, Syria was cleared of Egyptian troops and Ali agreed to restore the Turkish fleet, retaining (thanks to the intercession of the powers) his hereditary rights in Egypt.

France's return to the European Concert was formalised in July 1841 by her participation in the Straits Convention, signed by all five Great Powers. The Convention raised to the status of international law the so-called 'ancient rule of the Straits', which prohibited all foreign warships from passing through the Straits while Turkey was at peace. This was Russia's modest reward for agreeing to let the Treaty of Unkiar-Skelessi lapse and the price demanded for her cooperation with Britain in 1840. Clearly, the Russians attached great importance to ensuring that her Black Sea coast should not be open to attack by British or French warships in a conflict which did not involve Turkey. In practical terms, this meant that Britain could not retaliate against a Russian threat to India, or elsewhere, by despatching a naval force into the Black Sea.

The crisis of 1839–41 was a triumph for Palmerston's vigorous diplomacy which lessened Russian influence at Constantinople and French influence in the Levant. It also had a significant effect on international relations. Anglo-Russian cooperation became so cordial that the Tsar even proposed a secret alliance with Britain. Anglo-French relations, on the other hand, were seriously embittered by Thiers' insistence on backing Mehemet Ali. The estrangement was also unduly prolonged by Palmerston's delay in responding to French overtures for a *rapprochement*. His lack of generosity contrasted markedly with Metternich's sympathetic attempt to help France save face after Theirs' dismissal. The crisis of 1839–41 clearly contributed to the ending of the alignment of the Great Powers along ideological lines, a feature of the early 1830s, when the liberal entente confronted the conservative powers of the Holy Alliance. Even so, Anglo-French relations were being severely strained before 1840 by their rivalries in the Iberian peninsula, exacerbated by Palmerston's cavalier treatment of French interests. His successor as Foreign Secretary in the new government that came to power in 1841, Lord Aberdeen, was a much more conciliatory person. He succeeded in restoring the Anglo-French entente between 1841 and 1846, but his pliant nature led to dangerous misunderstandings in Anglo-Russian relations.

4 The Crimean War 1854–6

The Crimean War is usually regarded as an accident, as a war without intelligible causes, the product of misunderstandings and incompetence on both sides. This traditional view is well summed up in M. S. Anderson's verdict that: 'No state or statesman had wanted the war. All bore some responsibility for it.' Thus Russia's culpability lay in the fact that the Tsar made a series of blunders, rather than plotting the overthrow of the Ottoman Empire. Britain's responsibility stemmed from the errors of a weak and incompetent government, whose policy failed to deter the Russians from provocative steps while succeeding in encouraging the Turks to adopt an intransigent attitude to Russian demands. The French, for their part, were to blame for initiating the crisis in the Near East by reviving an old quarrel over the guardianship of the 'Holy Places' in Palestine.

This traditional interpretation of the origins of the Crimean War has been challenged by Norman Rich. Although he does concede that serious errors and miscalculations were made by both sides he nevertheless insists that the war occurred because certain groups and individuals wanted a showdown with Russia at this time. Chief among these were the Turks and Russophobic public opinion in Britain, aided and abetted by the former Foreign Secretary, Palmerston, and the British ambassador at Constantinople, Stratford de Redcliffe. This new interpretation obviously differs in important respects from the traditional 'consensus' that the war was an accident, even though it is not based on new evidence so much as on a re-assessment of the existing published sources. It is rather like re-reading a familiar story in which the roles of Red Riding Hood and the Wolf have been reversed!

The following explanation of the origins of the Crimean War is based, for the most part, on the more traditional view. Since the motives of the main participants in the crisis are now even more debatable than formerly, a brief summary of the sequence of events that led to Turkey (followed later by Britain and France) declaring war on Russia in 1853–4 may be helpful.

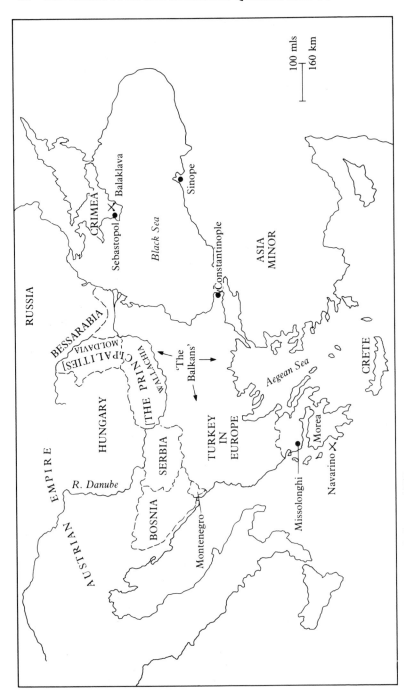

The Balkans and the Black Sea c. 1850

a) Events Leading to the Outbreak of War

The crisis in the Near East began in 1850 with a seemingly absurd dispute over the respective rights of the Latin (Catholic) monks as against the Greek (Orthodox) monks in the Holy Places in Palestine. The French success in this dispute – as champions of the Latin monks – in December 1852 led the Tsar to seek ways of putting pressure on the Sultan to acknowledge Russia's supposed right to be the protector of the Orthodox Church in the Ottoman Empire. When a special mission to Constantinople in the spring of 1853, led by Prince Menshikov, failed to secure satisfaction of Russia's demands the pressure on Turkey was stepped up. In July 1853, Russian troops occupied the Danubian principalities of Moldavia and Wallachia which acknowledged the Sultan's suzerainty. By this time, the British and French fleets had anchored outside the Dardanelles, as a gesture of support for the Turks. In an attempt to defuse the crisis Austria initiated a series of diplomatic moves to find a formula acceptable to both the Tsar and the Sultan. The Turkish rejection of the most important of these moves, the Vienna Note in August 1853, was a crucial stage in the deepening of the crisis. In October, Turkey declared war on Russia after the Tsar had rejected an ultimatum to evacuate the occupied provinces. The sinking of a Turkish flotilla at Sinope in the Black Sea in November 1853 created a storm of protest in Britain and France, whose governments were subjected to increasing pressure from public opinion – more especially in Britain – to stand firm against Russia. The hardening of attitudes led to the failure in late 1853 of further diplomatic efforts to find the elusive formula that would safeguard Turkey's integrity while satisfying the Tsar's honour. In March 1854, Britain and France signed an alliance with Turkey and declared war on Russia. Austrian persistence with further diplomatic efforts to end the conflict were unavailing until January 1856, when the Russians finally agreed to peace talks.

b) The Holy Places Dispute and the Menshikov Mission, 1850–3

Although the dispute over the guardianship of the Holy Places – which included such issues as which monks should hold the keys to the Church of the Nativity at Bethlehem – has been called a 'churchwardens' quarrel', it had serious implications. At root it was a question of whose influence prevailed at Constantinople – French or Russian, and so became a matter of prestige. In May 1850 the Sultan was presented with a French demand for the reinstatement of the full rights of the Latin monks as granted by the Capitulations, or treaty, of 1740. These rights had long fallen into disuse. A furious struggle lasted for over two years between French and Russian diplomats at Constantinople. The bewildered Sultan, a Muslim caught in the Christian cross-fire, resorted to duplicity, which only served to prolong and aggravate the crisis even though it could have been settled by compromise – the eventual outcome in April 1853.

The motives of Louis Napoleon, President and subsequently (from December 1852) Emperor of France, were twofold. He saw this question as a promising issue for causing a rift between Catholic Austria and Orthodox Russia and, by undermining the 'Holy Alliance', creating opportunities for French diplomatic initiatives in Europe. A more immediate consideration was to use the issue to secure the support of Catholic opinion in France – heedless of the warnings from London that 'the Holy Places question, if roughly handled, is one that may bring on trouble and war'. The Tsar, whose status or credentials as the protector of the Orthodox Church were much more genuine than Napoleon's, was obliged to support the pretensions of the Greek monks. As a British minister observed: 'it is one of those questions on which the moral power of the Emperor of Russia rests'. The Sultan's eventual decision in favour of the Latin monks, in December 1852, was therefore a grievous blow to the Tsar's prestige.

Turkey's usefulness to Russia lay partly in her role as a 'buffer', guaranteeing the immunity of Russia's southern coastline from attack by the western maritime powers. This had been based on the tacit understanding that the Turks feared Russia more than any other Great Power. In 1852, fear of France had induced the Sultan to give way to Louis Napoleon's demands – fear occasioned by a French threat to bombard Tripoli in North Africa, and the appearance of the latest French warship, the 90-gun *Charlemagne*, at Constantinople. The Turkish ministers calculated that the French fleet would outclass the combined Russian and Turkish fleets, and acted accordingly. The Russian Foreign Minister argued, not unreasonably, that if it was fear that had induced the Sultan to give way to France's demands, then fear of Russia was the weapon that had to be applied at Constantinople to reassert Russian influence there. Hence the decision to despatch a high-powered mission of naval and military chiefs, headed by Prince Menshikov, to the Porte in the spring of 1853.

In his determination to put pressure on the Turks, the Tsar made two fatal errors of judgement. Firstly, he believed that unrest in parts of the Ottoman Empire, especially a revolt in Montenegro, a small Balkan state, was a clear sign of Turkey's weakness. Secondly, he seriously misread the international situation. Not only did he believe that a perfect community of interest existed between Russia and Austria in the Near East, but he also assumed he could count on British support, an attitude encouraged after the pacific (and anti-Turkish) Lord Aberdeen had become Prime Minister in December 1852. In January 1853, the Tsar initiated a series of conversations with Sir Hamilton Seymour, the British ambassador to Russia. Reviving proposals he had made in 1844 in the course of a state visit to Britain, the Tsar suggested a 'gentleman's agreement' for dealing with the supposedly imminent

collapse of the Ottoman Empire, in cooperation with Britain, as shown
in the following extract from Seymour's report:

1   In the Turkish Empire are several millions of Christians whose
    interests I am called upon to watch over, while the right of doing
    so is secured to me by Treaty. I may truly say that I make a
    moderate and sparing use of my right . . .
5   Now Turkey, in the condition which I have described, has by
    degrees fallen into such a state of decrepitude that . . . eager as we
    all are for the continued existence of the man (and that I am as
    desirous as you can be for the continuance of his life, I beg you to
    believe), he may suddenly die upon our hands; we cannot
10 resuscitate what is dead; if the Turkish Empire falls, it falls to rise
    no more; and I put it to you, therefore, whether it is not better to
    be provided beforehand for a contingency, than to incur the
    chaos, confusion, and the certainty of a European war, all of
    which must attend the catastrophe if it should occur unexpected-
15 ly, and before some ulterior system has been sketched; this is the
    point to which I am desirous that you should call the attention of
    your Government.
       Sir, I replied . . . I would . . . observe, that deplorable as is the
    condition of Turkey, it is a country which has long been plunged
20 in difficulties supposed by many to be insurmountable.
       With regard to contingent arrangements, Her Majesty's Gov-
    ernment, as your Majesty is well aware, objects, as a general rule,
    to taking engagements upon possible eventualities, and would,
    perhaps, be particularly disinclined to doing so in this instance.
25   The rule is a good one, the Emperor replied . . . still it is of the
    greatest importance that we should understand one another, and
    not allow events to take us by surprise; 'now I wish to speak to
    you as a friend and as a gentleman; if we manage to come to an
    understanding on this matter, England and I, for the rest, it
30 matters little to me; I am indifferent as to what others do or
    think' . . .
       I am bound to say that . . . the Emperor is prepared to act with
    perfect fairness and openness towards Her Majesty's Govern-
    ment. His Majesty has, no doubt, his own objects in view; and he
35 is, in my opinion, too strong a believer in the imminence of
    dangers in Turkey. I am, however, impressed with the belief, that
    in carrying out those objects, as in guarding against those
    dangers, His Majesty is sincerely desirous of acting in harmony
    with Her Majesty's Government.

Most historians do not regard these 'Seymour conversations' as sinister
in intent, believing that the Tsar's main object was to stress his desire
for an understanding with Britain in the Near East. Not surprisingly,

however, some British ministers became very mistrustful of the Tsar's intentions, suspecting that he was aiming to destroy the Turkish Empire. Such suspicions were increased by the Tsar's plan to put pressure on Turkey. In January 1853, Russian troops were concentrated on the borders of Moldavia and Wallachia. In late February, Menshikov arrived in Constantinople with instructions to break off diplomatic relations with the Porte if Russia's demands were not accepted. These demands, contained in a detailed set of instructions prepared by the Foreign Ministry, focused on three issues. Firstly, the Sultan was to rectify the concessions made to the Latin monks which had damaged the Tsar's prestige as protector of the Orthodox Church. (This issue was resolved in late April by a compromise and ceased to be contentious.) The second demand was for a formal published Convention or treaty, incorporating Russia's existing rights and privileges in the Ottoman Empire. But the crucial demand was that this Convention should recognise Russia's right 'to make representations on behalf of the Orthodox Christians within the Ottoman Empire'. Since Orthodox Christians amounted to about one third of the Sultan's subjects, such a right, if conceded, would reduce Turkey to the status of a Russian protectorate. All historians agree that this was an unacceptable demand, constituting a serious threat to the independence of Turkey. Most contemporaries viewed it in a similar light, as giving Russia an undefined right of interference in the internal affairs of the Turkish Empire. Suspicion of Russia's intentions were thereby greatly increased.

In reality, contrary to the Tsar's belief, Russia did not enjoy any such existing rights under the treaties of Kutchuk-Kainardji (1774) and Adrianople (1829). The Russian Foreign Ministry had got it wrong, confusing rights over a new church to be built in Constantinople in the 1770s with a right to make representations on behalf of the inhabitants of the Danubian principalities, granted in 1829. The situation was further complicated by the fact that, under the so-called 'millet' system (a form of delegated authority) the Orthodox clergy exercised a political as well as religious influence over the Balkan Christians. A right or privilege granted to the Orthodox Church and/or its clergy therefore had implications which went beyond the spiritual realm. Consequently, a Russian claim to make representations on behalf of the Orthodox Church, clergy or Christians, was something of a political minefield. Once the suspicions of the Turks and their western sympathisers had been aroused by Menshikov's demands for a formal treaty, it mattered little that he was willing to scale down the substance of the demands to a more modest level – ultimately to little more than a face-saving formula. Russia was henceforth regarded by the Turks and others (including 'Mr Punch') as attempting to destroy the Turkish Empire, as shown in this extract from 'The Russian Lochinvar' which was published in *Punch* magazine:

1 The big-booted Czar had his eye on the East,
  For treaties and truces he cares not the least,
  And save his good pleasure he conscience hath none,
  He talks like the Vandal and acts like the Hun.
5 So faithless in peace here, and so ruthless in war,
  Have ye e'er heard of King like the big-booted Czar?

  He stayed not for speech, but, with sabre and gun,
  He rushed into Turkey, though cause there was none;
  But when he got near to the old Iron Gate,
10 He found certain reasons which urged him to wait.
  For down by the Danube stood Omar Pasha,
  Prepared to encounter our big-booted Czar.'

  So he drew up his legions – serf, vassal, and thrall,
  His footmen, and horsemen, and cannons, and all,
15 Then out spake bold OMAR, his hand on his sword,
  In an attitude fitting an Ottoman Lord,
  'O come ye in peace, or come ye in war,
  Or to see ST SOPHIA, you big-booted Czar?'

  'I've long asked your homage, my suit you denied,
20 And my holy religion you've scorned and decried,
  So now I've come down with this army of mine,
  The rights and the wrongs of the case to define,
  And you have not a chance, for the Mussulman star
  Must pale when it looks on the flag of the Czar.

Modern historians are not fully agreed in their interpretation of this complicated issue. Norman Rich, in particular, argues that obsessive Russophobes (such as Stratford de Redcliffe and Palmerston) deliberately misrepresented the nature of Russia's intentions with the aim of provoking war. Most writers, however, take the view that the Russians were to blame for creating an atmosphere of suspicion and mistrust. This was not related to the precise nature of the demands being made at a given moment from late February to May 1853, but owed much to Menshikov's deliberately overbearing manner, intended to intimidate the Turks. From the outset, when he insisted on the dismissal of the Turkish Foreign Minister, he attempted to dictate to the Turkish government, not negotiate with them.

The decision of the Turks (no doubt influenced by hopes of western support) to reject Menshikov's later, and more limited demands of early May, infuriated the Tsar. Faced with the choice of a humiliating climb-down or an increase in pressure on Turkey, he gave the order for Russian troops to occupy the Danubian principalities in July 1853. By the summer of 1853, therefore, the battle lines for the future conflict were being drawn. Turkish resistance to Russia's demands drew the

Tsar into a sharper confrontation with Turkey, while Britain and France committed themselves more deeply by moving their fleets to Besika Bay, just outside the Dardanelles. The use by three of the European powers of fleets and armies as diplomatic weapons, when none of them was seriously intending war, increased the danger of a conflict. Since direct Russo-Turkish negotiations had failed to solve the crisis, the best hope of a peaceful settlement lay with diplomatic intervention by the other powers. The time had come for Austria to play a leading role in the search for a formula that would satisfy the Tsar's honour while safeguarding Turkey's integrity.

c) The Failure of Diplomatic Efforts to Avert War, July–December 1853

Austro-Russian relations had been cordial for the previous 20 years but in 1853 Count Buol, the Habsburg Foreign Minister, was alarmed by the occupation of the Danubian principalities, bordering on the Austrian Empire. Austria was in a quandary. If she sided openly with the western powers, she ran the risk of attack by Russia across her vulnerable frontier. If, on the other hand, she supported Russia, she had reason to fear French hostility, directed at her Italian possessions. Buol's solution to this dilemma was to persist with mediation attempts from July to December 1853 and beyond.

One outcome of his efforts was the Vienna Note, a diplomatic formula agreed by representatives of the four powers meeting at Vienna in July 1853, to be recommended to the Tsar and the Sultan for their approval:

1 If the Emperors of Russia have at all times evinced their active solicitude for the maintenance of the immunities and privileges of the orthodox Greek Church in the Ottoman Empire, the Sultans have never refused again to confirm them by solemn acts testify-
5 ing their ancient and constant benevolence towards their Christian subjects. His Majesty the Sultan . . . inspired by the same dispositions, and being desirous of giving to His Majesty the Emperor of Russia a personal proof of his most sincere friendship . . . has been solely influenced by his unbounded confidence in
10 the eminent qualities of his august friend and ally, and has been pleased to take into serious consideration the representations which his Excellency Prince Menchikoff conveyed to him.

   The Undersigned has in consequence received orders to declare by the present note that the Government of His Majesty the
15 Sultan will remain faithful to the letter and to the spirit of the Treaties of Kainardji and Adrianople relative to the protection of the Christian religion, and that His Majesty considers himself bound in honour to cause to be observed for ever . . . the

enjoyment of the spiritual privileges which have been granted by
20 His Majesty's august ancestors to the orthodox Eastern Church,
and which are maintained and confirmed by him; and moreover,
in a spirit of exalted equity, to cause the Greek rite to share in the
advantages granted to the other Christian rites by Convention or
special arrangement . . .
25 The Sublime Porte, moreover, officially promises that the
existing state of things shall in no wise be modified without
previous understanding with the Governments of France and
Russia, and without any prejudice to the different Christian
communities.

Although Nicholas and the Turkish representative at Vienna
accepted the Note, the Sultan and his ministers regarded it as too
vaguely worded, thus permitting Russia to claim to act as protector of
the Orthodox Christians. When the amendments they insisted on were
subsequently rejected by the Tsar in September, this attempt by the
Great Powers to find a solution to the dispute suffered a major setback.

Most historians believe that the Turkish objections to the wording of
the Vienna Note were well-founded, especially in the light of its
subsequent interpretation by the Russian Foreign Minister. Nesselrode's so-called 'violent interpretation' of the Note certainly convinced
Clarendon, the British Foreign Secretary, who was no Russophobe,
that Russia did regard it as justifying her interference in Turkey's
internal affairs. The oft-repeated assertion that Stratford was to blame
for encouraging the Turks to reject this peace initiative is therefore seen
by most historians as of dubious validity and of little significance since
the Turks needed no persuading to reject it, if they valued their
independence. Once again, Norman Rich dissents from the 'consensus'
view. He not only cites evidence of Stratford's culpability but also
questions whether Nesselrode's interpretation of the Vienna Note
merits the description 'violent', given to it by Clarendon.

The failure of the Vienna Note weakened the collective stance of the
four Great Powers. While Austria and Prussia remained sympathetic to
Russia, Britain and France became more committed to Turkey's side,
sending their fleets forward to Constantinople. By mid-October, Turkish nationalist resentment at Russia's continuing occupation of the
Danubian principalities put the war party in the ascendant at Constantinople. Confident of western support, Turkey declared war on Russia in
October 1853, when the Russians refused to withdraw their troops from
Turkish territory. Thereafter, further diplomatic efforts to solve the
crisis were complicated by the repercussions of military action, especially the sinking at Sinope, in late November, of a Turkish flotilla
carrying troops to the Caucasus front. The British press (quite unfairly)
seized on this 'massacre' in which 4,000 Turks lost their lives, as a
demonstration of Russian treachery, fanning the flames of Russophobia

in Britain. The movement of the British and French fleets into the Black Sea in January 1854, a belated move to prevent another 'Sinope', in its turn had some influence on the Tsar's decision to reject a proposal for a six-power peace conference. After this set-back to diplomatic efforts to avoid war, there seemed little alternative for Britain and France but to support Turkey by declaring war on Russia in March 1854.

d) Responsibility for the War

The question of responsibility for the outbreak of the Crimean War has traditionally been answered by apportioning varying degrees of blame to all participants, within the overall context of the war as an accident. This view remains tenable, providing it is recognised that an alternative interpretation now exists which stresses the active desire for war against Russia of some individuals and groups in London and Constantinople. The net effect of this new approach is, of course, to shift a substantial amount of blame usually placed on Russia on to Britain.

Russia's main responsibility lay in the series of miscalculations and errors of judgement which resulted in a confrontation with Turkey from which it was difficult to extricate herself with honour. Despite

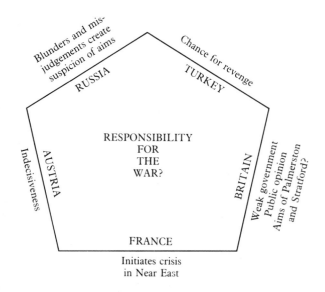

Responsibility for the Crimean War?

evidence to the contrary, the Tsar persisted in his belief that he could count on both British and Austrian goodwill. His conviction that Turkey was in a state of imminent collapse was also mere wishful thinking, leading to the assumption that the Turks could be bullied into accepting Russia's demands. In particular, the Menshikov mission has been called 'perhaps the most important step towards war taken by any of the states concerned'. Furthermore, the Tsar made no allowance for the powerful current of anti-Russian feeling which the Turkish government was eventually unable to control. Generated by Menshikov's behaviour, it reached fever pitch after the Russian occupation of the Danubian principalities. This military action itself raised the stakes in an already tense diplomatic crisis. Finally, it could be said that Nicholas' exaggerated sense of honour led him to reject several diplomatic attempts to resolve the crisis by compromise in late 1853. The Collective Note of late November–early December 1853 illustrates the efforts of the neutral powers to find a formula for resuming negotiations between Russia and Turkey:

1 The Undersigned, Representatives of Austria, France, Great Britain, and Prussia . . . have met together in Conference, in order to devise the means of reconciling the difference which has arisen between Russia and the Sublime Porte . . . [and] . . . have
5 resolved to offer their good offices to the two belligerent parties . . .
   The assurances given at different times by His Majesty the Emperor of Russia exclude, on the part of that august Sovereign, the notion of assailing the integrity of the Ottoman Empire. In
10 fact, the existence of Turkey in the limits assigned to her by Treaty is one of the necessary conditions of the balance of power in Europe . . .
   His Majesty the Emperor moreover has not confined himself to these assurances; he has declared that it never was his intention to
15 impose upon the Porte any new obligations, or any which might not be in conformity with the Treaties of Kutchuk-Kainardji and Adrianople, according to the stipulations of which, the Sublime Porte has promised to protect throughout its dominions the Christian religion and its churches. The Court of Russia has
20 added, that in requiring from the Ottoman Government a proof of its faithful adherence to former engagements, it by no means had the intention of diminishing the authority of the Sultan over his Christian subjects . . .
   The sentiments manifested by the Sublime Porte during the
25 recent negotiations prove, on the other hand, that it was prepared to recognise all its Treaty engagements, and to take into account, as far as its sovereign rights would allow, the interest felt by His Majesty the Emperor of Russia in a religion which is his own and

that of the majority of his people.

30   . . . In this state of things, the Undersigned are convinced that the . . . surest means of attaining the object desired . . . will be to make a joint communication to the Sublime Porte . . . to enable it to make known the conditions on which it would be disposed to treat.

There is general agreement among historians that the Tsar's blunders were almost equalled by those of the British government. The coalition government formed in December 1852 under Lord Aberdeen, with Clarendon as Foreign Secretary, is regarded as the weakest and most divided of all British cabinets of the mid-nineteenth century. Because of the rifts between, on the one hand, the pacific (and anti-Turkish) Aberdeen and Clarendon and, on the other, Russell (a prominent Whig) and Palmerston who pressed for a firm policy against Russia, the government frequently resorted to half-measures. For example, the despatch of the fleet to Besika Bay in June 1853, instead of to Constantinople, tended to encourage the Turks more than it deterred the Russians. Furthermore this weak government came under increasing pressure from the press, which gave full expression to the violent Russophobia that characterised public opinion after 1849, when Tsar Nicholas was nicknamed the 'gendarme of Europe'. Almost irrespective of the actual issues involved, British public opinion regarded Russia as a powerful and dangerous reactionary force whose supposed expansionist designs had to be resisted at all costs. Hence the popularity of Palmerston, whose antipathy to Russia at this time was well known. The role of Lord Stratford, ambassador at Constantinople, in encouraging Turkey to reject both Menshikov's demands and the Vienna Note has long been highly controversial. Although seemingly vindicated by a detailed study in the 1930s, he has been re-cast by Norman Rich (as noted earlier) as one of the major villains of the piece.

France's culpability lay mainly in initiating the crisis in the Near East by raising the issue of the Holy Places. Louis Napoleon has rightly been accused of 'playing to the gallery' at home, regardless of the likely repercussions on Russo-Turkish relations – for long a sensitive and dangerous issue in international relations. On the other hand, Napoleon III showed little desire to aggravate the crisis in 1853–4 and made several proposals designed to facilitate an honourable retreat by the Tsar. French policy was not motivated by hostility to Russia, but by Napoleon's desire to create a liberal alliance with Britain. If his ultimate objective was to destroy the 'Waterloo League' and the 1815 treaties, his immediate target was the Holy Alliance, especially the close association of Austria and Russia, which was in fact shattered by Austria's ultimatum to Russia to evacuate the Danubian principalities in June 1854.

The main criticism historians make of Austria's role in the origins of the Crimean War is the indecisiveness of Austrian policy in 1853–4. For too long she allowed the Tsar to persist in his mistaken belief that 'I can count on Vienna', as Nicholas insisted in late June 1853. In reality, the Russian occupation of the Danubian principalities was regarded as a serious threat to Austrian interests, especially her trade down the Danube. Although Buol deserves credit for his initiatives in seeking a diplomatic solution to the crisis (such as the Vienna Note) the fundamental aim of Austrian policy was to avoid taking sides, so as not to antagonise either Russia or France. Had Austria come out openly against Russia at an earlier date, the Tsar might have realised the need to tread more warily in his dealings with Turkey.

Although the Turks appeared, at times, to be the hapless victims of French and Russian power politics, they were by no means innocent of warlike intentions. The signs of western support in the mounting crisis of 1853 presented them with a unique opportunity to retaliate for the succession of defeats they had suffered at the hands of Russia since 1768, at roughly 20-year intervals. In the Holy Places dispute, the duplicity of the Turkish ministers was quite remarkable, secretly making concessions which nullified the privileges granted only days before to the other side. Far from encouraging a compromise solution, the Turks turned the dispute into an auction in which the rival bidders escalated their threats. The Sultan's rejection of the Vienna Note in its original form undoubtedly sabotaged the best hope of a peaceful solution and made war more likely. Whether the amendments insisted on by the Turks (and subsequently rejected by the Tsar) were justified by legitimate concern for their integrity, or whether they were intended to make war more likely, has re-emerged as a matter of dispute. The difficulty is that the correct interpretation of face-saving formulae is a rather elusive matter.

Even within the traditional view of the causes of the Crimean War, significant differences of emphasis have been attached by historians to the roles of the leading states, especially Russia. While some historians regard Russian policy as fundamentally defensive, others believe that the Tsar's constant talk of a partition of European Turkey indicates that he, if not his advisers, was contemplating an expansionist policy to secure substantial advantages for Russia.

e) Diplomacy and War, March 1854 to December 1855

In the spring of 1854, the diplomatic situation in Europe was very unusual. Four of the Great Powers were in basic agreement on the need to defend the integrity of the Ottoman Empire, but only two of them had declared war on Russia for the sake of protecting it. Prussia's reluctance to get involved in war with Russia is easy to understand since she had no direct interest in Near Eastern affairs at this time.

Furthermore, the Prussian King had no wish to antagonise the Tsar and in any case was notoriously indecisive. Austria's situation was rather different. As noted earlier, both her economic interests and her military security were threatened by the Russian occupation of the Danubian principalities. But, until the signing of an Austro-Prussian alliance in April 1854, Austria could not risk involvement in the east in case Prussia seized the opportunity to weaken Austrian influence in the west, especially in Germany. The alliance of 1854, however, gave Austria the confidence to demand that Russia evacuate the principalities. When the Russians withdrew in August 1854, the area was occupied by Austrian troops for the duration of the war, by agreement with Turkey and Russia.

Since Austria wished to avoid committing herself any further to the anti-Russian side, she took the lead in promoting diplomatic moves to end the war. The 'Four Points', accepted by the western powers in August 1854, remained as the basis of peace proposals for the duration of the conflict. The general objective of the proposals was stated to be 'to seek means for connecting the existence of the Ottoman Empire with the general balance of power in Europe'. Two of the four points dealt with Russia's claims to be the sole protector not only of the Orthodox Christians but also of the inhabitants of Serbia and the Danubian principalities, by substituting a collective guarantee of all the Great Powers. A third point dealt with free navigation of the mouth of the Danube, an issue of particular concern to Austria. The other point proposed a revision of the Straits Convention of 1841, initially 'in the interests of the balance of power in Europe'. This was a vague and fairly innocuous formula, but it was later defined in much more stringent terms as terminating Russia's preponderance in the Black Sea. This final point, implying severe restrictions on Russia's naval power, was the main sticking point in the subsequent negotiations.

The Tsar's rejection of the Four Points as 'injurious to Russia's interest and her honour' left Britain and France with two complementary courses of action: to exert pressure on Austria to side openly with them against Russia, and to force Russia to negotiate on the basis of the Four Points by inflicting military defeats on her forces. Both were pursued, with varying degrees of success, throughout the following year. For example, military setbacks induced the Tsar to accept the Four Points in late November 1854, but by this time Britain had decided to insist on stiffer terms regarding the Black Sea. Negotiations in the spring of 1855 also broke down over this point, so that renewed peace talks had to await further victories. More rapid success seemed to reward allied efforts to include Austria within the anti-Russian coalition. In December 1854, Austria signed a Tripartite Alliance but then managed to delay an ultimatum to Russia for a whole year!

The performance of the British army and, to a lesser extent, the much larger French forces in the Crimean War left much to be desired. The heroic, yet futile Charge of the Light Brigade, sent to capture the wrong guns, was but the most dramatic example of inept military command. The allies were fortunate, in fact, that the Russians displayed even greater military incompetence, as well as being hampered by extended overland supply lines, stretching over several hundred miles. The allied commanders had assumed that their main task was to prevent a Russian advance through the Balkans. The Russian withdrawal, however, obliged the allies to direct their main attack on the Crimea, a target favoured by some British leaders from the outset. The capture of the Crimean port of Sebastopol, the base of the Black Sea fleet, would destroy Russian naval power in the Black Sea, thereby eliminating a major threat to Turkey's security.

The failure of the allied commanders to follow up their initial successes in September 1854 with a rapid assault on Sebastopol proved a costly error. After the Russians, for their part, failed to dislodge the allied armies from the Crimea in the battles of Balaklava and Inkerman, military deadlock ensued from November 1854 to the following June. The winter of 1854–5 brought dreadful suffering to the allied troops, aggravated by medical and administrative incompetence, against which Florence Nightingale battled with great determination. (Her success is shown by the reduction in death from disease in the British army from 16,000 in the first half of the war to 2,000 in the remainder.) In the autumn of 1855, the reinforced allied armies defeated the Russian field army and, at long last, achieved their initial objective with the capture of Sebastopol.

The fall of Sebastopol in September 1855 was a serious setback for Russia but by no means amounted to a total defeat. The allies were therefore faced with the prospect of yet another campaign if they were determined to win a complete victory over Russia. By this time, however, Napoleon III no longer felt attracted to the idea of extending the scope of the war with the aim of liberating Poland and Finland, and effecting changes in Italy and along the Rhine. French public opinion felt that the capture of Sebastopol satisfied France's honour and wanted an end to the war, in tune with Napoleon who wanted to restore Franco-Russian relations by a moderate peace.

In Britain, on the other hand, Palmerston, who had replaced the incompetent Aberdeen as Prime Minister in February 1855, was still in a belligerent mood. Insisting on the need for what he called 'a long line of circumvallation to confine the future extension of Russia', he advocated campaigns in the Baltic and the Caucasus. His standpoint, shared by Clarendon, is explicable on the grounds that the military successes achieved by September 1855 scarcely justified the sacrifices made by Britain or entitled her to insist on severe terms of peace. His aggressive stance, although supported by British public opinion, struck no responsive chord in Europe, allowing Buol to resume his diplomatic

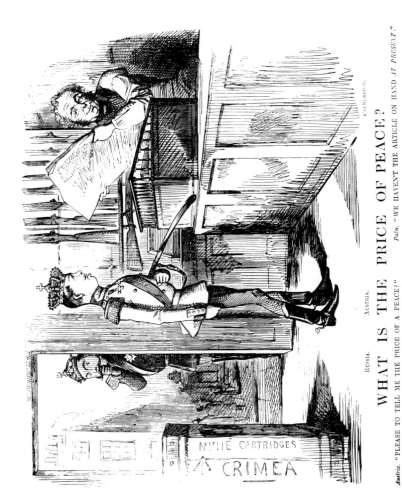

WHAT IS THE PRICE OF PEACE?

Austria. "PLEASE TO TELL ME THE PRICE OF A PEACE?"

Palm. "WE HAVEN'T THE ARTICLE ON HAND *AT PRESENT*."

Punch *cartoon, December 1855*

pressure on Russia to make peace. In December 1855 Austria issued an ultimatum, backed by Prussia, threatening Russia with war if she did not negotiate on the basis of the Four Points. Acceptance of the ultimatum by the new Tsar, Alexander II, in January was followed by an armistice and the opening of a peace conference in Paris in late February 1856, marking the end of the Crimean War.

f) The Treaty of Paris, 1856

At the peace conference, Napoleon III's desire to restore good relations with Russia, even at the expense of his entente with Britain, was very evident. The British consequently found themselves alone in pressing for severe terms which Russia was unlikely to accept. In fact, the British wanted the peace conference to fail, to justify extending the war against Russia, but the overwhelming desire of the other states for peace ensured the defeat of the British stratagem.

In general, the terms of the Treaty of Paris were an elaboration of the Four Points, proposed in August 1854. Russia's protectorship over the Danubian principalities and Serbia was replaced by a collective European one, while the existing rights and privileges of the Balkan Christians were guaranteed by a new reform edict issued by the Sultan. Turkey itself was admitted to the Concert of Europe, with a guarantee of her territorial integrity and independence. An international commission was set up to ensure freedom of navigation along the Danube. A modest territorial change also reduced Austrian fears of Russian interference with her Danubian trade. Southern Bessarabia (ceded to Russia in 1812) was restored to Turkey and incorporated into Moldavia. This arrangement had important commercial as well as strategic advantages for Austria, turning the Danube into a 'German river'. Russia's tactic of diverting trade through the port of Odessa by making the mouth of the Danube impassable for large vessels was thereby frustrated. The administration of the two Danubian principalities was to be reformed so as to create an 'independent national administration' under Turkish suzerainty, but the issue of uniting them (favoured by Napoleon) was left unresolved.

The most severe aspect of the treaty was the section designed to ensure that the Black Sea was neutralised. Russia was prohibited from maintaining warships or naval arsenals there, so that she could no longer threaten a sudden attack on Constantinople. Although the same restriction was applied to Turkey, the Russians regarded this limitation on their sovereignty as a grievous humiliation – to be reversed at the earliest favourable moment.

The Treaty of Paris was a major blow to Russian pride but it was, in general, a remarkably lenient peace settlement. Certainly, in the view of the British government it did not go anything like far enough to lessen the possibility of future Russian expansion. A tripartite alliance, signed

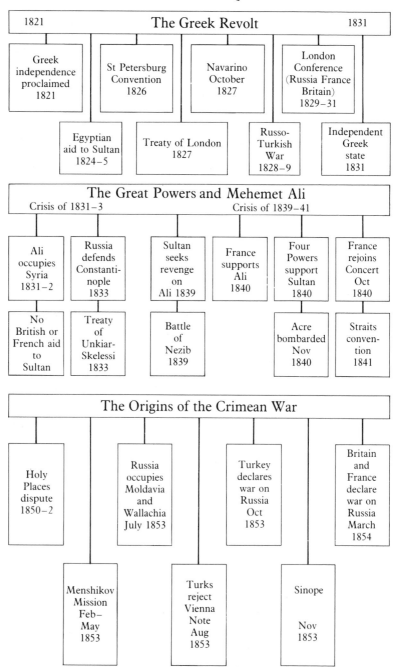

Summary – The Great Powers and the Eastern Question 1821–56

by Britain, France and Austria, to ensure Russia's adherence to the terms of the treaty was only effective as long as the three powers were willing to act in unison, which was not long. Although no major crisis arose over the Ottoman Empire during the next 20 years, no lasting solution to the Eastern Question, especially in terms of Turkish maladministration, was provided by the Treaty of Paris.

The Crimean War, A. J. P. Taylor suggests, was fought against Russia, not for the sake of Turkey. It served to check Russian expansionist ambitions for 20 years, but at a heavy cost in terms of lives and resources. The main impact of the war was therefore on the relations between the Great Powers and its damaging effect on the whole system of the Concert of Europe.

Making notes on 'The Great Powers and the Eastern Question'

You require three distinct but closely related sets of notes on this chapter. The first set will provide you with an overview of the topic. This will be in two parts:

1. An outline date chart showing the major events from 1821 to 1856. Compile this from the Summary (opposite). Remember to add the Treaty of Paris.
2. An answer to the question 'What was the Eastern Question?' and a summary of each of the Great Powers' interests in the fate of the Ottoman Empire. The information you need to do this is in section 1 of the chapter.

The second set will provide you with a record of events from 1821 to 1841. This will be in three parts:

1. The Greek Revolt 1821–31 (based on section 2 of the chapter).
2. Mehemet Ali and the Crisis of 1831–3 (based on section 3a of the chapter).
3. Mehemet Ali and the Crisis of 1839–41 (based on section 3b of the chapter).

For each part you will need three headings:

a) Background (What happened, excluding the part played by the Great Powers).
b) The involvement of the Great Powers.
c) The effect on Great Power relationships.

The third set will provide you with a record of the causes of the Crimean War. This will be in three parts:

1. Historical interpretations. Summarise the two interpretations described in the first three paragraphs of section 4.

2. The sequence of events. Compile a date chart based on the Summary on page 108 and on section 4a of the chapter.
3. Who was to blame? State your opinion on the ways in which each of the Great Powers, plus Turkey, was responsible for the outbreak of the war. The discussion in section 4d of the chapter will need to be supplemented by reference to sections 4b and 4c.

Answering essay questions on 'The Great Powers and the Eastern Question'

Most readers will be thankful that the majority of A-level essay questions set on this topic in the past have been relatively straightforward. This is perhaps a recognition that this large and complex topic presents enough difficulties to the student without the examiner adding to them! Frequently the approach adopted has been to pose a very general question that allows the candidate to select as he/she chooses from the large amount of relevant evidence that is available. In such cases it is particularly important to resist the temptation to present a narrative account of events. There is far too much to be told to fit into the time allowed. Selection is of vital importance.

Examples of typical questions are:

1. 'To what extent was the peace of Europe threatened by the Eastern Question in the period 1821 to 1841?'
2. 'In what ways did the decay of the Ottoman Empire affect international relations between 1821 and 1856?'
3. 'What were the long term causes of the Crimean War?'
4. 'Why was the Ottoman Empire of concern to the European powers in the period 1831 to 1856?'

In each of these cases it is relatively simple to plan an essay made up of a number of paragraphs, each of which presents a different answer to the question. Choose one of the questions and make a list of the main paragraph points you would use. Pay careful attention to the dates specified in questions 1, 2, and 4.

Occasionally 'challenging statement' questions are asked on the Eastern Question. For example:

5. 'Discuss the claim that "the Eastern Question in the period 1821–56 was essentially about the balance of power".'

Prepare to answer this question by carrying out the stages described on pages 36 and 57. Are there any assumptions or definitions that need to be explored in the introduction? The conclusion should do more than summarise the argument you have presented in the main body of the essay – although, of course, it should also do this. One of the aims of a conclusion should be to leave the reader with an interesting idea that is related to the topic but is not an integral part of your answer. Very often this is best done by drawing attention to some aspect of the topic that is outside the scope of the question. In the case of question 5, it might best be done by making a challenging statement of your own about the Eastern Question in the years between 1870 and 1914. This you should be able to do once you have read *Rivalry and Accord: International Relations 1870–1914* in this series.

Source-based questions on 'The Great Powers and the Eastern Question'

1 The Treaty of Kutchuk-Kainardji, 1774
Carefully read the extracts from the treaty given on pages 81–2. Answer the following questions.
a) What is meant by 'Ministers of that Empire' (line 12)? (2 marks)
b) What territory was restored to the Ottoman Empire by the treaty? (3 marks)
c) What rights, with regard to religion, were given to Russia by the treaty? (5 marks)
d) How valid was the Russian claim to the protectorship of all Orthodox Christians within the Ottoman Empire, based on this treaty? Explain your answer. (5 marks)

2 The Seymour Conversations, 1853
Carefully read the extracts from Sir Hamilton Seymour's report, given on page 95. Answer the following questions:
a) What was the Tsar's proposal? (3 marks)
b) What reasons did Seymour give the Tsar for not wanting to take the proposal further? (2 marks)
c) Assess the reliability of Seymour's report. (6 marks)
d) What miscalculations of the situation does the report portray the Tsar as making? (4 marks)

3 'The Russian Lochinvar'
Carefully read the extracts from the poem 'The Russian Lochinvar' published in *Punch* in 1853. Answer the following questions:
a) Is the author of the poem friendly or hostile towards the Tsar? Provide three pieces of evidence to support your answer. (7 marks)
b) What is the author's attitude towards the Turks? Support your answer with evidence. (4 marks)
c) What was the significance of poems such as this in the lead-up to the outbreak of the Crimean War? (4 marks)

4 Attempted mediation, 1853
Carefully read the extracts from the Vienna Note of July 1853 (pages

98–9) and from the Collective Note of November–December 1853 (pages 101–2). Answer the following questions:
a) The Vienna Note was the draft of a document that Britain, France, Austria and Prussia hoped would be issued by whom and having been accepted by whom? (2 marks)
b) Why was this diplomatic initiative unsuccessful? (6 marks)
c) What was the intention of the Collective Note? (2 marks)
d) Why did this not lead to peace between Russia and Turkey? (3 marks)
e) Identify the similarities in the tone of the two documents. (7 marks)

5 What is the price of peace?
Carefully study the *Punch* cartoon of December 1855 reproduced on page 106. Answer the following questions:
a) The artist communicates his true meaning by the way he chooses to represent each of the three characters. For each character describe how he is portrayed and the meaning the viewer is intended to gain from his portrayal. (15 marks)
b) Why was Palmerston not prepared in December 1855 to consider peace with Russia? (5 marks)

CHAPTER 6

The Decline of the Concert of Europe 1856–70

1 The Effect of the Crimean War on International Relations

The Crimean War was preceded by almost 40 years of peace, but was followed by 14 years of intermittent warfare from 1856 to 1870. The objective of these wars was to accomplish what the 1848 revolutions had failed to achieve – the revision of the 1815 settlement to the advantage of some states, rather than in the interests of Europe as a whole. This was a period when phrases such as 'the healthy egoism of states' and '*realpolitik*' were used to justify expansionist aims. Two major territorial changes took place during this period. Firstly, the unification of Italy under Piedmont, a process begun by the Franco-Piedmontese war against Austria in 1859. Secondly, the creation of the German Empire under Prussia by means of Bismarck's three wars, against Denmark in 1864, Austria in 1866 and France in 1870–1.

The Great Powers acting in concert in the interests of 'Europe', a striking feature of international relations in the period 1815–54, was not much in evidence from 1856 to 1870. Although several congresses were proposed during these years, only two took place: one on the Schleswig-Holstein dispute in 1864 – a failure, and one on Luxembourg, a face-saving operation for Napoleon III in 1867. Historians are generally agreed that a major explanation for this marked contrast in international affairs between the early and later nineteenth century is that the Crimean War was an important watershed. One symbol of this change is the fact that Austria was the only Great Power in 1857 still committed to the defence of the status quo in Europe.

Many historians also emphasise the importance of Austria's role in the Crimean War as a key factor in the disintegration of the Holy Alliance. The ultimatum to Russia in June 1854 (to evacuate the Danubian principalities) combined with her second ultimatum in December 1855 (to make peace) has even been regarded as a 'turning point' in European history, on the grounds that it ended the friendship and cooperation of the two eastern conservative powers and began an era of hostility that lasted until 1914.

A major consequence of the Treaty of Paris of 1856 was a change in the priorities of Russian foreign policy, in the sense that defence of the status quo in Europe was relegated to second place after 1856. Thereafter, the prime aim of Russian diplomacy was to remove the humiliating restrictions imposed on Russian naval power in the Black Sea. Russia was therefore a 'revisionist' force in international affairs, seeking ways to undo the 1856 settlement. She was even prepared to countenance changes in the 1815 settlement if her own interests were not directly threatened. This was a far cry from the role of 'gendarme of Europe', attributed to Nicholas I in 1849. Russian policy was also influenced, at least for several years after 1856, by animosity towards Austria for her 'betrayal' in joining the 'Crimean Coalition' against her. Consequently, the Tsar would not veto changes to the 1815 settlement which adversely affected Austria as a Great Power. As A. J. P. Taylor has observed: 'Metternich's system depended on Russia's guarantee; once that was withdrawn, the system could be overthrown'. In the period 1856–70, Russia aligned herself with France until 1863, and later with Prussia, both of whom were pursuing anti-Austrian policies.

Russian ministers were also acutely conscious of the weakness of the Tsarist regime in the 1860s. The shame of defeat led to preoccupation with the need for modernisation and reform in Russia but these very reforms (especially the abolition of serfdom) had a destabilising effect on the country. Despite this, Russia continued to play a prominent role in European diplomacy after 1856, but she was untypically anxious to avoid confrontation or war with another Great Power.

France was regarded as the real victor of the war since she had played a larger and more glorious military role than Britain. Napoleon III's prestige was high – making him the 'Arbiter of Europe' from 1857 to 1863 and enabling him to champion the cause of 'nationality'. Unlike his uncle, Napoleon I, his preferred method for restoring France's greatness and creating a French hegemony in Europe was diplomacy, not war. Napoleon was not out to destroy the Concert but his attempts to revise the 1815 settlement by conferences were opposed by the other Great Powers, suspicious of his aims. Although Franco-Russian relations were often quite cordial after 1856 (except during the Polish revolt of 1863) France failed to secure a firm alliance with Russia because their interests did not sufficiently coincide. The problem was that Russia demanded France's full support in the Near East (which would jeopardise Napoleon's relations with Britain) while France was mainly preoccupied with the prospects for expansion and with threats to her security in western Europe.

Although Britain was also a victor in the Crimean War, she had little reason to be proud of her performance. It was felt that her sacrifices of men and money had achieved little. This led to disenchantment with active involvement in European affairs, which became quite a marked feature of British opinion in the 1860s. This was a major change in attitude since Britain had been a prominent member of the Concert before 1856. The Crimean War also ended Anglo-Russian cooperation in international affairs, which had been a valuable source of strength to the Concert since 1841.

For Austria the Crimean War was a disaster. Not only did she alienate Britain and France by her hesitant policy during the war but she also angered Russia by her 'betrayal' in eventually joining the 'Crimean Coalition'. Austria was therefore in a very exposed and vulnerable position in 1857 as the only remaining active defender of the status quo and lacking the support of the Holy Alliance. Her expectation that it could be revived in 1860 at the Warsaw meeting of the three conservative monarchs was quite unrealistic – a feature of Austrian diplomacy throughout this period.

Prussia emerged with little glory from the war and suffered the humiliation of being excluded from most of the sessions of the Congress of Paris. On the other hand, her passive role during the war meant that, unlike Austria, she had avoided alienating Russia.

2 Other Influences on International Affairs 1856–70

Although the Crimean War undoubtedly had an important influence on European diplomacy it would obviously be absurd to maintain that it was the only factor responsible for the decline of the Concert and for the changes that took place between 1856 and 1870.

Domestic factors, as always, had a major influence on the attitudes and policies of the Great Powers. In Russia, as noted above, modernisation and reform combined with financial problems led to a cautious approach to foreign affairs. In France, Napoleon III's sensitivity to public opinion had an important influence on decision-making. This was especially the case in the 1860s, when economic difficulties reduced the popularity of the regime at a time when liberalisation of the political system made it easier for Napoleon's opponents to voice their discontent with his domestic and foreign policies. A major casualty of the liberalisation process was the unorthodox financial methods (such as 'deficit financing') hitherto used by the government to foster economic expansion. Deprived of this means of overcoming the business recession, the regime floundered. Until the introduction of dramatic political changes in 1869–70 which created the so-called 'Liberal Empire', Napoleon III relied heavily on an active foreign policy as a way of boosting his flagging prestige. In Britain, an almost opposite economic situation led to the adoption of a very passive foreign policy. Preoccupation with industrial growth and the expansion of overseas trade fostered an increasing indifference amongst politicians and public opinion to political problems on the continent. This attitude, openly espoused by the Conservatives, further weakened the influence which Britain had previously exerted in European affairs, already undermined by Palmerston's unsuccessful attempt to deter a Prussian attack on Denmark by sheer bluff in 1864 (see page 123). In Prussia, a serious political crisis continued from 1862 to 1866 over her parliament's refusal to vote the funds for military changes demanded by the King. This had a direct bearing on the policies pursued by Bismarck, appointed Minister-President in 1862.

Other factors which were important to the success of Bismarck's policies were the steady growth of the Prussian economy in the 1850s, the accumulation of financial reserves and the introduction of military reforms that made the Prussian army the most efficient in Europe. Austria, by contrast, experienced none of these benefits so that the concept of 'Dualism' – the sharing of influence over the German Confederation between the two German powers – no longer accorded with the realities of power politics. Financial weakness and military backwardness seriously undermined Austria's position as a Great Power. The burden of sustaining the policy of 'armed mediation' in 1855 had even led the government to sell off the Austrian state railways to raise more funds for the army.

Three other factors unrelated to the Crimean War are worthy of note. Firstly, Napoleon III's restless ambition which created great unease in the capitals of Europe. Secondly, Bismarck's belief in *realpolitik* – policies based on realism, not clouded by sentiment, which he conducted with a ruthlessness for which most of his contemporaries were unprepared. Finally, Austria's pursuit of a 'policy of illusions' – refusing to make concessions in good time and failing to see the need to secure alliances to stave off disaster. Much of this seems to have been related to the Emperor's stubborn sense of honour, which made flexible diplomacy almost impossible.

3 The Great Powers and Italy, 1859–61

In 1856 the Vienna settlement was still largely intact as regards Italy. Yet within a few years it was mostly destroyed, and although the unification of Italy was not fully completed until 1870, most of Italy was united under Victor Emmanuel, the Piedmontese King, by 1860.

A united Italy was not the aim of either Napoleon III or Cavour, Prime Minister of Piedmont, but the Franco-Piedmontese alliance of 1858, concluded secretly at Plombières, initiated a chain of events that neither of them could fully control. The agreed object of the alliance was to evict the Austrians from Lombardy and Venetia and to set up a Kingdom of North Italy under Victor Emmanuel. Whereas Cavour had hopes of adding the central duchies (Parma, Modena and Tuscany) and part of the Papal States to north Italy, Napoleon's idea was to form a separate kingdom out of the duchies to be ruled by his nephew, who was to marry Victor Emmanuel's daughter. Napoleon's motives were a mixture of generous intentions, self-seeking and power politics. He genuinely wished to 'do something for Italy', secure Italian gratitude and obtain Savoy and Nice for France as payment for his services, while undoing the 1815 settlement.

Napoleon had no cause to fear Russian support for Austria because in March 1859 the Tsar promised benevolent neutrality in the war, as part of a Franco-Russian understanding in European affairs. Britain was also well disposed towards Piedmont (which had contributed 15,000 troops to the Crimean Coalition in 1855) – at least as long as the Whigs

THE GIANT AND THE DWARF.

"BRAVO, MY LITTLE FELLOW! YOU SHALL DO ALL THE FIGHTING, AND WE'LL DIVIDE THE GLORY!"

Punch *cartoon, June 1859*

were in office. Then, with the tension mounting between Austria and Piedmont in 1859, the Austrians made the crass error of rejecting a conference on Italy unless the Piedmontese demobilised their army.

The 'War of Liberation', however, failed to go according to plan. Napoleon agreed to a truce when only Lombardy had been liberated, partly because of heavy casualties and partly because Prussia adopted a threatening attitude. Rather late in the day 'that ignominious scum of Prussia', as Franz Joseph called her, finally rallied to Austria's side and mobilised her army as a warning to Napoleon to cease the conflict with Austria. Meanwhile the Habsburg princes were evicted from the duchies, which voted for union with Piedmont. But the main danger to the Italian cause arose when Garibaldi launched a freebooting expedition to Sicily and Naples which threatened to provoke intervention by Prussia and/or Russia. Piedmontese troops occupied the Papal States to forestall a possible attack by Garibaldi, following which plebiscites produced a vote for union with Piedmont. The Kingdom of Italy which emerged in 1860–1 was far from the modest little state that Cavour and Napoleon had conspired to produce.

  * That the Great Powers did not intervene to prevent this wholesale destruction of the Vienna settlement is evidence of the decline of the Concert. France was naturally reluctant to turn against her erstwhile ally to stop Garibaldi reaching Naples. Napoleon had agreed to the union of the duchies with the north, in return for Cavour's acceptance of his claim to Savoy and Nice, which he had forfeited by failing to liberate Venetia. Austria was reluctant to attack the Piedmontese, and perhaps the French, without assistance from either Russia or Prussia. The Tsar strongly disapproved of Garibaldi's attack on the Kingdom of Naples, but not to the point of taking active measures against the Italians. Moreover, Napoleon hastened to assure the Tsar that France would not permit an attack on Venetia and promised full French support for Russian interests in the Near East in the event of a 'catastrophe' there. The Austrians therefore came away empty-handed from the Warsaw meeting of the three conservative monarchs in October 1860. Had their hopes of a revival of the Holy Alliance been realised, the outcome of the Italian situation would have been very different.

The Whig government (led by Palmerston with Russell as Foreign Secretary) in Britain was not sympathetic to Austrian rule in Italy, believing that Austria should have seized the chance to acquire Moldavia and Wallachia (in exchange for Lombardy and Venetia) as proposed at the Congress of Paris in 1856. Even so, the scale of the changes taking place in Italy in 1860 caused some alarm but British policy failed to keep up with the pace of events. Russell put a good face on the final outcome by a famous despatch in October 1860, which referred to 'the gratifying spectacle of a people building up the edifice of

FREE   ITALY (?)

Punch *cartoon, July 1859*

their liberties and consolidating the work of their independence'. At least, the new Kingdom of Italy – proclaimed in March 1861, from which only Venetia and Rome were excluded – would not be dominated by France. It also had a good chance of being more stable under the dominance of the Piedmontese than in the past, under Austrian tutelage. Nevertheless, the unification of Italy completed what the Crimean War had begun: the destruction of the European order.

4 The Polish Revolt of 1863

In Poland, Russian rule had become more relaxed since the accession of the new Tsar, Alexander II in 1856. However, the minor concessions granted had encouraged nationalist hopes of more fundamental changes. The revolt began with a rising in Warsaw triggered off by the levy of a new batch of recruits for service in the army. It quickly spread throughout Poland. Unrest had been mounting since 1861, as Polish nationalists responded to modest liberalisation measures by demanding further concessions from the Russian-dominated government. Violent demonstrations in Warsaw and the attempted assassination of the Tsar's brother, recently appointed as Governor-General, were followed by repression and executions. This led to the formation of a radical revolutionary movement in Poland -- which the conscription of young men from Warsaw and the large towns was designed to break. The revolt took the form of guerrilla bands operating in the countryside, who held down the Russian forces of 150,000 men for about a year. However, the revolt failed for the same reasons as in 1830 – divided leadership and the lack of peasant support, as well as numerical inferiority to the Russian forces in Poland.

Diplomatic protests by the other Great Powers at Russia's treatment of 'Congress Poland', created in 1815, were unlikely to be effective unless they were well coordinated and, perhaps, backed by the threat of force. Since both Austria and Prussia had Polish provinces they were unlikely to support moves that might encourage Polish aspirations for independence. In fact, Prussia sided openly with Russia by concluding the Alvensleben Convention in early 1863 which permitted Russian pursuit of rebel refugees crossing into Prussia. Austria adopted an ambivalent position, refusing to coordinate her mild reproof with the western powers' more strongly worded protest to Russia. Even so, Britain and France failed to act effectively in unison. Napoleon's proposal for pressure on the Prussians was rejected in favour of a direct protest to Russia, and his subsequent suggestion in November 1863 for a European Congress to discuss Poland and other contentious issues was curtly rejected by the British. With Britain and France in such disarray, Russia had no need to fear naval action in the Baltic or the despatch of a French army to Poland.

The Polish crisis had quite a pronounced effect on international relations. It marked the end of the Franco-Russian alignment that had existed since 1859 and soured relations between Britain and France to such an extent that cooperation in the next crisis in 1864 was most unlikely. The Polish affair also demonstrated Bismarck's desire to establish closer ties between Prussia and Russia, which became the key alignment amongst the Great Powers for the rest of the decade. 1863 definitively marked the end of 'the Napoleonic Age' begun in 1857, and ushered in 'the Age of Bismarck'.

5 The Great Powers and Bismarck's Wars 1864–70

Between 1864 and 1871 the Prussian army fought three successful wars against Denmark, Austria and France. After the Danish war in 1864 the duchies of Schleswig-Holstein were surrendered to Austria and Prussia. The defeat of Austria in 1866 enabled Bismarck to set up a North German Confederation, dominated by Prussia. The war against France in 1870–1 facilitated the incorporation of the independent south German states (including Würtemberg and Bavaria) into a unified German state. The German Empire proclaimed in 1871 was, in this sense, the product of 'blood and iron'.

The conflict with Denmark was not directly related to the issue of German unity, but Bismarck's success in resolving the dispute over the duchies of Schleswig-Holstein, to the exclusive advantage of Prussia, was a remarkable demonstration of his ability to exploit the errors of his opponents. The problem arose over the attempt by the King of Denmark to alter the status of the two duchies, which were attached to the Danish crown by a Personal Union. The King, Christian IX, put himself in the wrong by incorporating Schleswig (with its large Danish population) into Denmark in November 1863, thereby violating the 1852 Treaty of London. The Austrians, for their part, were enticed into cooperating with Prussia instead of supporting the policy of the Federal Diet, by Bismarck's astute move in taking his stand on 'treaty rights' – a stance that Austria herself usually adopted. This separated her from the German princes and German liberal/nationalist opinion, which advocated the creation of an independent state of Schleswig-Holstein within the German Confederation.

As regards the other Great Powers, Bismarck correctly judged that while they might protest at Austro-Prussian military action against the Danes, they would not actively intervene on Denmark's side. Following the Austro-Prussian invasion of Denmark, the duchies were surrendered to Austria and Prussia in October 1864.

Bismarck's aim was to annex Schleswig-Holstein to Prussia, a solution unacceptable to Austria, so the fate of the duchies became a contentious issue between the two German powers in 1865–6. This served Bismarck's purposes well, because he seems to have concluded in the course of 1865 that the aim of establishing a north German union under Prussian domination – his minimum programme for solving the issue of German unity – probably necessitated war against Austria. This meant that from October 1864 to June 1866 Bismarck was engaged in an attempt to isolate Austria, so that the Prussian army had to fight only Austria and her German allies when war began in June 1866. After the defeat of the Austrian army at Sadowa in early July, the German Confederation was dissolved and replaced by a North German Confederation. This was dominated by an enlarged Prussia, which annexed several smaller states outright, but the four south German states retained their independence. Since Austria had to cede Venetia to Italy she ceased to be either an Italian or a German power.

The scale of Austria's defeat in June 1866 created great alarm, especially in France. Napoleon's critics asserted that 'it was France that was beaten at Sadowa', implying that, having failed to assist Austria, France had missed the chance to check the growth of Prussian power. Napoleon's ideas for securing compensation for France as a sort of 'consolation prize' for Prussia's aggrandisement in 1866 produced a minor crisis in 1867. His attempts to obtain Luxembourg for France were clumsily executed but his plan to purchase the duchy from the King of Holland was, it seems, thwarted deliberately by Bismarck. After this Franco-Prussian confrontation, war seemed only a matter of time. When the war began in July 1870 France found herself alone against the Prussians, just as Austria had been in 1866. Once again, Bismark had succeeded in isolating his opponent. On the outbreak of war Bismarck acted to discourage sympathy for France by releasing to the press evidence of French designs on Belgium and Luxembourg, dating from a draft treaty of 1866. Even before the final peace treaty was signed, the German Empire, now including the south German states, was proclaimed in the Hall of Mirrors at Versailles.

  * The unification of Germany under Prussia was made possible by the military superiority of the Prussian army over the Austrian and French armies. It also owed much to two other factors: Bismarck's remarkable diplomatic skill and unusually favourable circumstances in international relations. Bismarck's success as a diplomatist lay in his ability to confuse or deceive his opponents as to his ultimate objective by simultaneously pursuing alternative strategies. This enabled him to isolate his intended 'victim'. His success was also facilitated by the reluctance of the other Great Powers to act together to check Prussian aggrandisement. In brief, the Concert of Europe was enfeebled by the fact that in the 1860s Russia was revisionist, France expansionist and Britain almost isolationist.

The failure of the Concert to intervene effectively in the Schleswig-Holstein dispute in 1864 is not altogether surprising. It was a complicated question but the fate of the duchies was not a major issue and, although Britain wanted the dispute to be settled by the decision of the five Great Powers, no consensus emerged at the London Conference held from April to June 1864. Furthermore, although Palmerston had implied that Britain would support Denmark, this was bluff. Without French or Russian backing there was little that Britain could do. Yet Palmerston offered no inducements to either government that would secure their support in a question of little interest to them. France saw no reason to antagonise Prussia for the sake of pleasing Britain who had rejected her initiatives for helping the Poles in 1863. Russia, for her part, no longer attached great importance to maintaining the status quo for its own sake, however much she disliked Prussia's methods. On the other hand, the Concert did succeed in resolving the Franco-Prussian confrontation over Luxembourg in 1867, after the British government had summoned a conference on the issue. This defused the crisis, by producing a face-saving formula – but no territorial gain – for France.

The two wars fought by Prussia against Austria and France clearly represented a major challenge to the existing balance of power. Certainly, the changes in central Europe that resulted from the Austro-Prussian war virtually destroyed the Vienna Settlement of 1815, which the Concert of Europe was designed to uphold. Despite Austrian appeals to the other Great Powers for aid in the interests of the balance of power in Germany and in Europe, she was left to her fate.

* This raises the question why there was no intervention by the other Great Powers, acting either in concert or as individual states.

The simplest explanation is that Austria once again pursued a policy of illusions in refusing to recognise the need to make some concessions. A proposal for a European conference, made by Russia, Britain and France in May 1866, was sabotaged by Austria herself, who made it a pre-condition for attending the conference that there would be no discussion of territorial changes. Since the point of the conference was to avoid the impending war by timely concessions by Austria, there was little chance of the Concert, in the form of a five power meeting, being able to resolve the crisis. Even so, the possibility remained of diplomatic intervention backed by the threat of force by Russia, France or Britain, singly or collectively, for the sake of the balance of power. In fact, of the three neutral powers the only one likely to take sides was France, since both Russia and Britain were determined to maintain their neutrality and would go no further than offer 'friendly advice' to the Prussians to avoid war.

Russia's attitude is the more surprising since she was formerly the champion of 'Dualism' in German affairs and, at times, an arbiter between Austria and Prussia. The Russian view of the situation is made clear in the Memorandum drawn up by the Foreign Minister, Gorchakov, in September 1865. In this, Russia's dislike of Prussian ambitions and methods is balanced against the advantage of a strong Germany as a guarantee against western intervention in Poland. In addition, there was no clash of interests between Russia and Prussia in the Near East, whereas Austria had been unwilling to support Russian policy on some minor aspects of the Eastern Question in the 1860s. Above all, Gorchakov concluded, Russia needed peace to implement internal reform.

In Britain there was a reaction against the policy of 'menaces never accomplished and promises never fulfilled' that Palmerston had pursued ignominiously during the Danish crisis. The prevailing view in London was that Britain had nothing to fear from Protestant Prussia and that a strong Germany would be a useful bulwark against French expansion in Europe. British governments had become very mistrustful of France's ambitions after her acquisition of Savoy and Nice in 1860 – suspecting, not without cause, that Napoleon had designs on Belgium and/or the Rhineland. By 1865 cooperation with France in European affairs was not eagerly sought because Anglo-French relations had deteriorated further after the failure to support each other in the crises over Poland and Schleswig-Holstein. The breakdown of the Anglo-French alliance in 1863–4 has been seen as a 'landmark in the history of European diplomacy' by W. E. Mosse. Just as Britain could play only a modest part in the affairs of the continent without French support, so Napoleon III could no longer aspire to be the arbiter of Europe without Britain's backing.

By 1865 Britain was adopting a passive, non-interventionist posture towards continental affairs. In attacking Palmerston's policy of 'meddle and muddle' in 1864, the Tories asserted that Britain's national interest lay outside Europe and that the doctrine of the balance of power was 'founded on the obsolete traditions of an antiquated system'. The Conservative governments of the period from June 1866 to December 1868 refused to accept the responsibilities and commitments necessary to defend the status quo, but the attitude of many leading Liberals was not very different. It was after all Clarendon, the Liberal Foreign Secretary, who refused to participate in mediation between the German powers on the grounds that 'neither England's honour nor England's interests' were involved.

France's attitude to the impending Austro-Prussian conflict was unduly (and unwisely) influenced by Napoleon's desire to secure Venetia for Italy. Austria's refusal (until too late) to agree to its surrender forfeited French and British goodwill. It also led to Italy's alliance with Prussia in March 1866, obliging the Austrians to fight on two fronts. The expected Austro-Prussian conflict placed Napoleon in a serious dilemma. Sentiment led him to sympathise with Prussia as the agent of German national feeling. Calculation, on the other hand, dictated that if Prussia became more powerful then France should also make some territorial gain, such as Belgium or the Rhineland. Napoleon's discussions with Bismarck at Biarritz in October 1865 were inconclusive, partly because Napoleon thought he could get a better price for his neutrality if he waited. When this proved to be a mistake, his last-minute alliance with Austria did not oblige France to take part in the war.

Although the neutral powers had failed to prevent the outbreak of war in 1866 it was possible that they might attempt to influence the peace settlement. They could claim the right to be consulted about territorial arrangements within the German Confederation which had been established by the Great Powers at the Treaty of Vienna. Furthermore, Napoleon, having decided against armed intervention, insisted on playing a mediating role in the preliminary peace talks but Britain resisted pressure from Austria and Russia to participate in three-power mediation. The new Conservative government, intent on pursuing a non-interventionist policy, rejected the proposal arguing that the 1815 treaties were no longer binding.

That the Concert of Europe was not completely defunct after the war of 1866 was proved by the successful conference on the Luxembourg crisis in 1867. But Britain's reluctance to accept the responsibilities of a Great Power was shown by her public assertion that she would not honour the guarantee of Luxembourg's neutrality if it should be threatened in the future. This conference was the last meeting of the Concert before the outbreak of the Franco-Prussian war in July 1870.

There were two main reasons, perhaps, why the three neutral powers did not act in concert to prevent a conflict between France and Prussia in the years 1867 to 1870. Arguably, the nature of the tension did not lend itself to a settlement by negotiation at a conference. Napoleon's regime needed a boost to its prestige which could come only from a diplomatic victory over Prussia or from territorial gain. But German territory in the Rhineland was clearly not on the agenda while Britain would veto France's acquisition of Belgium. Equally, Bismarck's problem with the south German states was not so much a question of opposition to their unity with the north at the international level as the growth of 'anti-Prussianism' within the southern states. To overcome this he needed to raise a 'national issue' – such as war against France.

Another obstacle to concerted action by the neutral powers lay in their lack of agreement on other issues in international affairs from 1866 to 1870. In the Near East a number of relatively minor crises exerted a disproportionately large influence on international relations, especially on Russia's relations with Austria and France. A rising in Crete in favour of union with Greece in 1866 was followed by the threat of a rising of Balkan states against Turkish rule in 1867–8. These dangers to peace in the Near East made Russia unduly alarmed about Austria's alleged designs on Bosnia (see map on page 92) and anxious for diplomatic support. Negotiations with France, who was equally anxious for support against Prussia, foundered on the lack of common ground. Russia therefore turned to Prussia and reached an informal agreement in March 1868, by which each government would concentrate 100,000 men on either the French or the Austrian frontier in the event of Franco-Austrian military operations directed against Prussia or Russia. This agreement was held to imply that Russia would not oppose the completion of German unification.

After the failure of their negotiations with Russia, the French pursued extended talks with Austria and Italy in the hope of creating an anti-Prussian alliance. However, the presence of French troops in Rome, protecting the Pope against the Italians, was a barrier to success there, while the French badly misjudged the worth of Austrian protestations of goodwill. The reality of Austria's situation was that she would not risk another clash with Prussia unless and until France demonstrated her ability to emerge victorious.

A last-minute attempt to secure concerted intervention by the three neutral powers was made by Russia in early August 1870 to prevent the total destruction of the existing balance of power which was presaged by Prussia's early victories over the French. However, at the news of a major disaster for the French army at Sedan, in early September, the Russians abandoned their attempts at mediation by the neutrals. At the end of October they announced the abrogation of the Black Sea clauses, but agreed to attend a conference in London in January 1871 which conceded their demands, while asserting the principle that treaties could not be broken unilaterally. There was, however, no European intervention to save France from humiliating peace terms whose severity shocked the neutral powers. As Thiers, a leading Frenchman who had unsuccessfully toured the European capitals in search of a mediator, remarked: 'he could not find Europe'.

6 Conclusion: The Concert of Europe 1815–70

The nature of the Concert of Europe is hard to pin down because the Concert was a concept, an ideal which lacked precise meaning. Its elusive nature has been explained by some historians as stemming from the fact that it was based upon attitudes of mind rather than on precise institutional forms. As a French historian observed in 1909: 'it could not achieve the status of a regular and permanent institution; it could only be a more or less fortunate expedient, capable of resolving on occasion difficulties or problems which affected the interests of all'. But, as Gladstone, the leader of the Liberal party in Britain in 1879 remarked, 'common action means common objects'.

What were the 'common objects' that might provide the basis for cooperation among the Great Powers? The fundamental aim that could unite them in 1815 was the desire for international peace and stability. This was hardly surprising after the upheavals of the previous 20 years. Nor was it at all strange, after their experience of French hegemony in Europe, that the essential pre-requisite for peace and stability should be seen as an acceptance of the balance of power as a fact of life in international affairs. It seemed to the leaders of the victorious nations in 1815 that a rough equality of power existed among the five leading states and that this was a desirable thing to preserve – a 'just equilibrium', in short. So, despite being an abstraction, many European statesmen appealed to the Concert as representing a moral force superior to the national interests of individual states.

Obviously, the continuance of the Concert was dependent on a consensus among the Great Powers that the balance of power existing in 1815 should be preserved. The threat to this consensus came from France and Russia after 1815. French statesmen argued that the other Great Powers had extended their boundaries between 1789 and 1815 whereas she was confined to her 1790 frontiers by the Vienna Treaty. Russia's grievance was less obvious but she maintained that Britain's insistence on setting limits to Russia's accretion of power in Europe was inconsistent with her own continuing global expansion. The danger of a Franco-Russian combination to upset the 1815 balance surfaced periodically from 1815 to 1830, much to Metternich's alarm. It was successfully contained by the device of 'grouping' these two states within the framework of a five-power alliance, stabilised – until 1820 at least – by Anglo-Austrian cooperation.

However, a passive acceptance of the existing balance of power was, by itself, not enough to ensure peace and stability in Europe. It also required a consensus that an increase in territory or political influence by any one state was not permissible unless consented to by the other Great Powers. This attitude had also to be buttressed by a willingness to participate in collective action to check any attempts at aggrandisement. The point was made quite well by Lord John Russell in a speech in 1852:

1 We are connected, and have been for more than a century, with
  the general system of Europe, and any territorial increase of one
  Power, any aggrandisement which disturbs the general balance of
  power in Europe, although it might not immediately lead to war,
5 could not be a matter of indifference to this country and would,
  no doubt, be the subject of conference, and might ultimately, if
  that balance was seriously threatened, lead to war.

Two further requirements for peace and stability were restraint in the pursuit of national interests and respect for treaties. For example, the British and French governments did not give aid to the Polish insurgents in 1830 or the Piedmontese in 1848–9, despite strong pressure from public opinion to do so. Russia, for her part, could have extracted more concessions from the Turks than she did in the Treaty of Unkiar-Skelessi of 1833.

The maintenance of peace and the balance of power, therefore, were based on the three principles of national self-restraint, respect for treaties, and a willingness to enforce the decisions of the majority by concerted action. The latter was important since without it the Concert would have been greatly enfeebled. The successful solution of the Belgian problem in 1830–1 clearly necessitated coercion of the King of Holland by Britain and France, acting on behalf of the five Great Powers. Similarly, the ending of the Mehemet Ali crisis of 1839–41 depended on the defeat of the Egyptian forces by Anglo-Austrian and Turkish troops. The enforcement of the collective decision of four of the powers resulted in the Straits Convention of 1841, which is widely regarded as one of the greatest triumphs of the Concert of Europe in the nineteenth century.

* What type of forum was best suited to achieving the aim of peace and stability in Europe after 1815? If international cooperation was to be successful, the statesmen of Europe needed a *modus operandi* – a suitable mechanism for operating the ideal of the Concert. The first experiment, the Congress System, rapidly became committed by 1820 to the preservation of not just the balance of power but also of the status quo throughout Europe. The breakdown of the system by 1823 demonstrates that this was too rigid a form for the Concert to take. A more flexible approach, sometimes referred to as 'Conference Diplomacy' was successfully adopted to deal with the Belgian revolt in the 1830s. In essence, this amounted to a general agreement that defence of the major features of the 1815 settlement might be reconciled with changes to the precise arrangements made in the treaties, providing the consent of all the Great Powers could be obtained. Negotiations conducted through an ambassadorial conference proved to be a successful way of securing the assent of the Great Powers. This more flexible approach to international problems was also found to be effective in dealing with that most persistent source of tension amongst the Great Powers in the nineteenth century – the Eastern Question. In 1841, the powers, after a serious breach with France the previous year, re-affirmed the notion of a public law of Europe, in the form of the Straits Convention.

* Clearly, finding the right mechanism for international cooperation would have served little purpose if the Great Powers habitually adopted entrenched attitudes towards the problems that arose. The Concert of Europe was inevitably vulnerable to deadlock caused by dissent on ideological grounds. This became clear in 1820 at Troppau and in the resultant grouping of the Holy Alliance powers, reinforced by the Münchengrätz Agreement of the three Northern Courts in 1833. The 1830 revolution naturally exacerbated this ideological divide between the liberal western states and the conservative, or reactionary, eastern states. The fact that the Concert did not disintegrate after 1823 and again after 1830 demonstrates the value which the Great Powers placed on the continuance of cooperation. In fact, an important factor in the survival of the Concert was the flexibility of alignments within the ranks

of the five Great Powers which cut across the ideological divide. Examples of this include Anglo-Russian cooperation in the Near East in 1827–30 and in 1839–41, and attempts at Franco-Austrian cooperation in Switzerland and Italy in 1846–7. The flexibility of alignments was therefore a valuable lubricant to the mechanism of the European Concert. However, it was not a substitute for the three principles suggested above as necessary requirements for the maintenance of peace and stability in Europe. This is shown by the fact that the alignments of the Great Powers became even more flexible after 1856, but the Concert itself was then in decline.

   * That the Concert was in serious decline after the Crimean War seems indisputable. The reluctance of Britain and Russia, who were both in their different ways adversely affected by the war, to play an active part in European affairs from 1856 to 1870 was fatal to the working of the Concert. As the 'peripheral powers', their contribution to peace and stability in Europe after 1815 had been of major importance, as was highlighted in 1848–9. The Crimean War destroyed the consensus of the Great Powers. By 1857 Austria was the only state still committed to the defence of the status quo in Europe. Britain increasingly ceased to play an active part in continental affairs, while Russia adopted an opportunistic, 'revisionist' policy towards events in Europe. As Gorchakov, the Foreign Minister after 1856 put it, 'Russia is not sulking; she is silently biding her time'.

   Gorchakov shared with Bismarck and Cavour an indifference to the 1815 settlement, with which they had no personal ties. The leaders of Prussia and Piedmont also rejected respect for treaties, national self-restraint and stability, in favour of *realpolitik* and the 'natural egoism' of states – in other words the law of the jungle. The purpose of diplomacy itself underwent a sea change in the hands of Cavour, Napoleon III, and Bismarck. For them it was a preparation for war, not a means of avoiding it. Alliances were therefore concluded for aggressive, not defensive, purposes. The pact between Napoleon and Cavour at Plombières in 1858 has been aptly described as the 'first deliberate war plot in the nineteenth century'. Similarly, the alliance between Italy and Prussia in 1866 was based on the assumption that Prussia would provoke a war with Austria within a few months.

   The Concert did not cease to exist after 1856. Two conferences were held, in 1864 and 1867, and several more were proposed. However, the very fact that proposals for a conference were rejected by one or more of the Great Powers seems to underline the fact that the Concert had lost its former vitality. In rejecting Napoleon's suggestion for a congress in 1863 to include the Polish issue, Lord John Russell was overly explicit in his reply:

   1 Her Majesty's Government would feel more apprehension than confidence from the meeting of a congress of sovereigns and

ministers without fixed object ranging over the map of Europe
and exciting hopes and aspirations which they might find them-
5 selves unable either to gratify or to quiet.

The Queen of Holland's reaction to this reply was quite telling: 'It is the
death blow of an alliance which ought to have . . . managed the affairs
of the Continent, and secured us an era of peace'.

That France should want to destroy the Vienna Settlement, symbol
of her defeat and humiliation in 1815, was understandable. Clearly,
however, Napoleon III miscalculated the risks for France from undermining the Concert. That Bismarck should seek to destroy the German
Confederation and the existing balance of power in central Europe was
also hardly surprising. It was, therefore, the failure of the other Great
Powers to intervene, perhaps by collective mediation or even at the
stage of the peace settlement following the wars of this period, that
dealt a grievous blow to the Concert of Europe. Clarendon explained
the British government's unwillingness to act to prevent the impending
Austro-Prussian war in a letter to Queen Victoria in late March 1866,
from which this extract is taken:

1 Lord Clarendon ventures to express the opinion . . . that although
we might join with France in mediation . . . yet that we could not,
even in conjunction with France, use the language of menace
which might entail the necessity of action, first, because the time
5 for such action is gone by; we might have gone to the defence of
Denmark when she was attacked by Austria and Prussia, but it
was wisely determined that such a war ought not to be under-
taken. Secondly, because, England having acquiesced . . . in the
Treaty by which Austria and Prussia obtained possession of the
10 duchies, it is for Germany . . . to assist Austria in doing right and
to settle the duchies in the manner conformable to the wishes of
the inhabitants. Thirdly, the case is one in which neither English
honour nor English interests are involved. We have spoken in
defence of right; we cannot actively interfere with those who are
15 quarrelling over the spoils . . . The country would not tolerate any
direct interference in a quarrel with which we had no concern;
and all those . . . who attended the Cabinet on Thursday last,
expressed themselves in the strongest terms against it . . .

After 1870 the European Concert survived mainly as a mechanism for
resolving the problems arising from the decline of the Ottoman Empire
and, on one occasion, the 'Scramble for Africa'. When Gorchakov
conceded that 'the Eastern Question is not German nor Russian, but
European', he was acknowledging that Russia was obliged to show
some restraint in its dealings with Turkey for the sake of preserving
peace among the European Great Powers. That the idea of the Concert

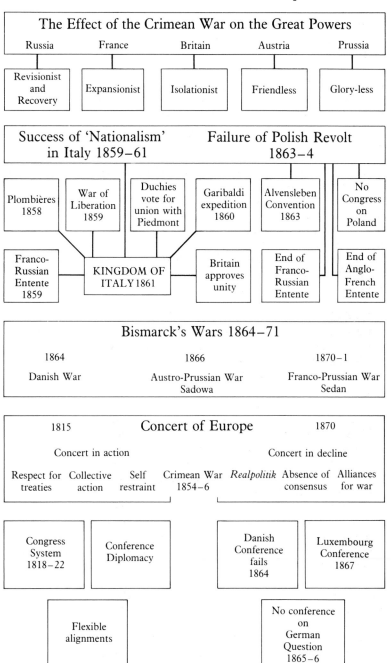

The Effect of the Crimean War on the Great Powers

Russia	France	Britain	Austria	Prussia
Revisionist and Recovery	Expansionist	Isolationist	Friendless	Glory-less

Success of 'Nationalism' in Italy 1859–61   Failure of Polish Revolt 1863–4

Plombières 1858	War of Liberation 1859	Duchies vote for union with Piedmont	Garibaldi expedition 1860	Alvensleben Convention 1863	No Congress on Poland
Franco-Russian Entente 1859	KINGDOM OF ITALY 1861		Britain approves unity	End of Franco-Russian Entente	End of Anglo-French Entente

Bismarck's Wars 1864–71

1864	1866	1870–1
Danish War	Austro-Prussian War Sadowa	Franco-Prussian War Sedan

1815   Concert of Europe   1870

Concert in action				Concert in decline		
Respect for treaties	Collective action	Self restraint	Crimean War 1854–6	*Realpolitik*	Absence of consensus	Alliances for war

Congress System 1818–22	Conference Diplomacy		Danish Conference fails 1864	Luxembourg Conference 1867
	Flexible alignments		No conference on German Question 1865–6	

Summary – The Decline of the Concert of Europe 1856–70

as a force for good in international affairs in general was not completely dead after 1870 can be seen from this extract from a speech by Gladstone, the Liberal leader in 1879:

1 In my opinion the third sound principle (of foreign policy) is this
   – to strive to cultivate and maintain, ay, to the very utter most,
   what is called the concert of Europe; to keep the Powers of
   Europe in union together. And why? Because by keeping all in
5 union together you neutralise and fetter and bind up the selfish
   aims of each . . . [Others] have selfish aims, as . . . we in late years
   have too sadly shown that we too have selfish aims; but their
   common action is fatal to selfish aims. Common action means
   common objects; and the only objects for which you can unite
10 together the Powers of Europe are objects connected with the
   common good of all.

However, it has to be said that Gladstone's idealistic desire to revive the Concert as an active force in European affairs made him almost unique among the political leaders of Europe in the late nineteenth century. More typical of the prevailing attitude amongst them is the view expressed in 1882 by the former Conservative Foreign Secretary, Lord Salisbury, when he said: 'in a matter not concerning a Musselman [Muslim] people . . . I believe the European Concert is rather a phantasm'.

Making notes on 'The Decline of the Concert of Europe, 1856–1870'

Your notes on this chapter should equip you to answer three possible questions:

1. *When* did the Concert of Europe decline?
2. *Why* did the Concert of Europe decline?
3. *How far/to what extent* did the Concert of Europe decline?

In order to answer the first question you will need to understand the chronological 'shape' of the period 1856–70. Compile a date chart for these years, using the middle three elements of the Summary on page 131 to provide the titles for your entries. Further details can be found, as required, in sections 3, 4 and 5 of the chapter.

In order to answer all three questions you will need to clarify your thinking on:

4. What was necessary for the Concert of Europe to operate effectively? (See the first part of section 6 for this.)
5. When, why and how far did these conditions cease to apply? (Sections, 1, 2, and 6 will provide you with ideas on this.)

You will probably find it easiest to organise your thinking on question 5 as a number of answers to 'why' (each starting with 'because'), with 'when?' and 'how far?' answered as supplementary points in each case.

Source-based questions on 'The Decline of the Concert of Europe, 1856–1870'

1 The Great Powers and Italy

Carefully study the two cartoons from *Punch*: 'The Giant and the Dwarf' and 'Free Italy (?)', reproduced on pages 117 and 119. Answer the following questions:
a) Who are the five characters represented in the cartoons? (5 marks)
b) What point is the cartoonist making in 'The Giant and the Dwarf'? Did events prove him right? Explain your answer. (5 marks)
c) In 'Free Italy (?)' what is the implication of Napoleon III being portrayed holding the papal tiara over Italia's head? (6 marks)
d) In 'Free Italy (?)' why is Venetia portrayed as it is? (2 marks)
e) What evidence is there to suggest that the two cartoons were drawn by the same person? (2 marks)
f) What is the cartoonist's attitude towards France? Justify your answer. (5 marks)

2 Britain and the Concert of Europe

Carefully read the extracts from Russell's speech of 1852 and his reply of 1863 to Napoleon III on pages 127 and 129–30, Clarendon's letter of 1866 to Queen Victoria on page 130 and Gladstone's speech of 1879 on page 132. Answer the following questions:
a) Which two of the extracts are generally in favour of British participation in the Concert of Europe? Which extract comes closest to arguing for an isolationist position? (3 marks)
b) Would it be fair to describe the views expressed by Russell in 1852 and 1863 as contradictory? Explain your answer. (7 marks)
c) What are the major purposes of Clarendon's letter to Queen Victoria? (3 marks)
d) What aspects of continuity and change in British foreign policy in the period 1852 to 1879 do the extracts illustrate? (7 marks)

Further Reading

Although useful information about the problems that faced statesmen can be found in general histories of nineteenth-century Europe, they often lack full explanations of policies and attitudes to such problems. A notable exception to this and a well written account is:

J. A. S. Grenville, *Europe Reshaped 1848–1878* (Fontana 1976).

A brief introduction to international affairs can be found in **Gordon Craig**'s chapter 'The System of Alliances and the Balance of Power' in:

J. P. Bury (ed.), *The New Cambridge Modern History, 1830–1870* (CUP 1960).

Two excellent works published more recently have greatly enlivened the study of international relations after 1815:

A. Sked (ed.), *Europe's Balance of Power 1815–1848* (Macmillan 1979) and **F. R. Bridge & R. Bullen**, *The Great Powers and the European States System 1815–1914* (Longman 1980).

Although they are both quite detailed and tend to assume some prior knowledge they well repay the effort involved in reading them, especially some of the stimulating essays in the **Sked** volume. Insight into the strengths and weaknesses of the Great Powers is provided by Chapter 4, 'Industrialization and the Shifting Global Balances, 1815–85' of:

P. Kennedy, *The Rise and Fall of the Great Powers* (Unwin Hyman 1988 and Fontana Paperback 1989)

For Italian and German unification, not covered in any detail in this book, the two volumes in this series by **Andrina Stiles** can be read with profit. An excellent discussion of Austria's problems (including the Metternich era and 1848) can be found in:

A. Sked, *The Decline and Fall of the Habsburg Empire 1815–1918* (Longman 1989)

Finally, no student of diplomatic history should deny him/herself the delight of at least sampling:

A. J. P. Taylor, *The Struggle for Mastery in Europe 1848–1918* (Oxford 1954).

Despite being confusing and provocative, it remains a stimulating, magisterial study of the follies of statesmen.

Sources on 'The Concert of Europe'

Useful source material, of varying quality, can be found in the following:

1. **R. Albrecht-Carrie**, *The Concert of Europe 1815–1914* (Harper 1968);
2. **K. Bourne**, *The Foreign Policy of Victorian England 1830–1902* (Oxford 1970);
3. **M. S. Anderson** (ed.), *The Great Powers and the Near East 1774–1923* (Arnold 1970);
4. **M. Walker** (ed.), *Metternich's Europe* (Macmillan 1968).

The latter ranges widely from 1815 to 1848 but some of the extracts are rather diffuse. Carrie's extracts are a bit 'dry'; Bourne's make more interesting reading, but the scope is limited to British policy.

Acknowledgements

The publishers would like to thank *Punch* magazine for permission to reproduce the copyright illustrations on pages 106, 117 and 119.

Index